A Taste of Prince Edward County

A GUIDE TO THE PEOPLE, PLACES & FOOD OF ONTARIO'S FAVOURITE GETAWAY

WRITTEN BY **CHRIS JOHNS**

PHOTOGRAPHY BY **JOHNNY C.Y. LAM**

ppetite
by RANDOM HOUSE

Appetite by Random House® and colophon
are registered trademarks of Penguin Random
House LLC.

Library and Archives of Canada Cataloguing in
Publication is available upon request.

ISBN: 9780147530684
eBook ISBN: 9780147530691

Cover and book design by Leah Springate
Food styling by Ruth Gangbar
Illustrations by Kate Golding
Map on page 18 by Kyle Topping

Printed and bound in China

Published in Canada by Appetite by Random
House®, a division of Penguin Random House LLC.

www.penguinrandomhouse.ca

0 9 8 7 6 5 4 3 2 1

appetite
by RANDOM HOUSE

Penguin
Random
House

THIS BOOK IS FOR JILLIAN AND HARPER
AND THE START OF OUR ADVENTURE IN THE COUNTY.
—CJ

TO ALL THE KIND AND GENEROUS SOULS,
WILD HEARTS AND HARDWORKING HANDS OF
PRINCE EDWARD COUNTY, PAST AND PRESENT.
—JL

Contents

FOREWORD

David McMillan, Co-owner of Joe Beef,
Liverpool House & Vin Papillon

The moment I cross the bridge over the Bay of Quinte, a warm sense of "I've been here before" comes over me. The déjà vu feels like a familiarity with the spirits, the ancestors, the landscape and the trees of this slice of Canadiana. I've lived in France, and my whole career has been spent working in Montreal, but the county, although it's not my home, feels like home.

When Chris told me he was writing this book I immediately said: "I want to contribute something." I've known him for a long time, ever since we first opened Joe Beef, and I can't think of anyone better suited to do justice to this place that neither of us are from, but both love. And I can't imagine a better pairing for Chris's writing than Johnny's photographs. Johnny's a transplant, as is most everyone who hasn't been here for 10 generations or more, but he knows the county, its people and its rhythms as well as anyone, and his images capture the essence of this special place.

I have met a vast collection of friendly, like-minded people in the county: hard workers, dreamers, farmers, every one of them with a deep love of this island that feels forgotten somewhere in time. There are the born-and-bred county folks who have been here for generations, who know every road, every pasture and every family. Then there are the newcomers: the people who picked up from wherever they lived, who saw what I see, and ultimately made significant life changes to move to the county. For so many, this is a place where people can come to start anew, be part of something, and work and contribute to the community.

And whether I'm talking to longtime locals or brand-new residents, I have great discussions all over the county. I often find myself dwelling on the idea that I work and live in Montreal in a very urban setting, but enlightening exchanges in the city are few and far between. I find myself craving the county and those conversations at the Legion, or the various watering holes around the island, on main streets or at wineries. I always feel the need to get one point across during these chats. In almost every conversation, you'll hear me say: "Do you realize how lucky you are to live here and be a part of what is going on?" I usually follow up by stressing how jealous I am of the beauty that fills the eyes and hearts of this amazing

community. Prince Edward County, to me, offers a chance to start a community or join an existing, robust one, and that isn't something that happens everywhere or every day.

I've driven along every road and explored every corner of the county during my stays. I fantasize about opening a restaurant, a B&B, a cider house, a winery, of farming goat or lamb. But I can also support, tour, explore and live the county life through visits, too, and I hope you will do the same with this book at your side. Visit Prince Edward County! #CountyUp

ROGERS' GOLDEN SYRUP

ROGERS' GOLDEN SYRUP

ROGERS' GOLDEN SYRUP

ANTIQUES ARE
NOT FOR SALE

Sugar Molds

HISTORY

The last time the great Laurentide Ice Sheet peeled back from the earth, some 14,000 years ago, there was nothing but water where Prince Edward County stands today. The whole peninsula was deep beneath the waves of a vast proglacial body of water known as Lake Iroquois. Slowly, over the next few millennia, the lake drained, first revealing the county's highlands as distinct islands, before eventually tracing out the shores of what we now recognize as Prince Edward County.

Around that same time the first Paleo-Indians arrived, chasing after the caribou, mastodons and mammoths they hunted. Eventually, a few plucky Mound Builders (so-named for the burial mounds they left behind) came on the scene. Many of them were nomadic and just passing through, fishing and hunting and navigating the waterways, but some stayed put and were probably the first to plant crops in county soil. The Iroquois who followed formed the first villages and cultivated the three sisters: corn, beans and squash, a legendary trio of plants that grow so beautifully together, one sustaining the other, they were considered gifts from the gods.

The first European to glimpse the limestone cliffs of the county was

Étienne Brûlé—a great French explorer whose story ends with him being murdered and eaten by the Huron tribe he was accused of betraying—who paddled past here at the start of the seventeenth century. Samuel de Champlain, Brûlé's superior, arrived in the Bay of Quinte area as part of a Huron war party, in 1615. Fifty years later, Jesuit and Sulpician explorers started setting up missionaries in the Cayuga village of Kenté near Lake Consecon.

Following the Battle of the Plains of Abraham in 1759, and the subsequent signing of the Treaty of Paris, the British took possession of much of Eastern Canada. Consequently, when British Loyalists—American Colonists loyal to the British crown—were driven out during the American Revolutionary War, many of them fled north to Canada. The first of these United Empire Loyalists began arriving in the area now known as Marysburgh in 1784.

Granted 100 acres, an axe and a kettle, it was tough going for those early settlers who had no real experience with homesteading. Undaunted, and with little choice in the matter, they set about clearing land and banded together to build simple log cabins, barns and churches.

Thick forests of maple, white and red cedar, juniper, willow and white pine covered the region at the time and provided the first source of industry for the area. By July of 1792, when Lord Simcoe officially established the boundaries of Prince Edward County, naming it after the fourth son of King George III, Prince Edward Augustus, the settlers were reasonably well established and logging in earnest. Scott's Mill on the Black River in Milford, site of the county's first town hall, was up and running around 1815.

By the mid-nineteenth century, though, the great primeval forests that once covered the area were essentially gone, turned over to farmland. Wheat, much of it shipped to Great Britain, was one of the first successful agricultural exports, but it was another kind of grass that would change the county's fortunes.

The period between 1860 and 1890 in Prince Edward County is known as the Barley Days. Barley and hops—a member of the Cannabaceae family of plants—are crucial ingredients in the brewing of beer and both grow exceptionally well in the rich limestone soil of Prince Edward County. American brewers in and around New York long considered the county's malting barley to be among the best, so when a 400 percent tax was placed on American whiskey (to raise money for the civil war) in 1861, the fortunes of many farmers were made. At the peak of

the Barley Days, the county was shipping 50,000 bushels a day. In a good season a farmer could pay off his entire mortgage.

To get all of this barley across Lake Ontario, schooners were needed and a substantial shipbuilding industry grew to meet the demand. Once again fortunes were made and the hard life of the first settlers was left behind, if not entirely forgotten. For 30 years, the county grew and prospered. In 1890, though, the party came to a crashing halt. The introduction of the McKinley tariff, a 48.4 percent tax on agricultural imports to the United States, caused the price of barley to crash almost overnight and the market disappeared.

Farmers largely abandoned barley and turned to more diversified crops, but shipbuilding continued to be buoyed by the steady growth of the fishing industry. By the mid-1800s, commercial fishermen were pulling millions of pounds of whitefish, trout, perch and pickerel out of Lake Ontario every year and sport fishermen came from around the world to try their luck in the same waters. It was a dangerous business, however, and commercial fishing vessels make up the bulk of the sunken wrecks that ring the waters around the county.

In 1882, George Dunning, a plant nursery salesman, introduced a new, much safer business idea to the region. Dunning was inspired by a demonstration of the latest fruit and vegetable canning technology he'd seen at the Philadelphia Food Exposition, so he approached Wellington Boulter, a wealthy insurance executive, with the idea to build an experimental canning factory in Demorestville. The first shipment of canned goods left the Picton railroad station bound for British Columbia in 1888. By 1900, canned products from the area were being shipped around the world. There were some 50-odd canning companies around by 1915, and more than 25,000 acres of cropland under contract to supply them. Millions upon millions of cans: tomatoes, peas, creamed corn, pears, plums, apples and cherries were shipped over the coming years, earning Prince Edward County the title "The Garden County of Canada."

Throughout the first half of the twentieth century, canning remained a lucrative industry, but eventually competition from large multinationals, increased regulation and the introduction of frozen food as a viable alternative started to take their toll. Slowly but surely the old canning factories closed shop, with the last one ceasing production in 1996.

Before that, another, considerably more daring—not to mention illegal— industry would make its mark on the county: one that relied, once again, on water instead of rail to support it.

While the temperance act in Ontario made the consumption of liquor illegal between 1916 and 1927, it was still possible to make alcohol for the purpose of export. Consequently, the introduction of Prohibition in America in 1920 meant that more than a few dashing county characters saw the opportunity to make their fortune—and fame—as rum runners. Main Duck Island, a few short kilometres from the American border, became a hub and Claude "King" Cole, the farmer and fisherman who owned the land, operated a whole crew of smugglers. Racing through the night across treacherous waters, in often unpredictable weather, outsmarting the well-armed American coast guard, and getting rich doing it, made the exploits of men like Bruce Lowery, "Peg Leg" Jones and "Wild Bill" Sheldon the stuff of county legend.

Things settled down for a while after Prohibition was repealed, and through much of the twentieth century the county got quiet but never lost its agricultural identity.

Tourism started becoming a bigger factor with the arrival of places like the exotically named Palace-of-the-Moon dance-hall pavilion, and the expansion of Lakeshore Lodge. In 1959, Outlet Provincial Park was opened and three years after that, Sandbanks. The two would eventually combine into the park

we have today. Today, it attracts more than half a million visitors each year and those numbers are only increasing.

The 1980s saw the return of vinifera grapes to the county. This area may be Ontario's newest wine region, but they've been growing award-winning wine around here for nearly 150 years. Admittedly, there was a pretty big gap after 1876 when one Norland Doxon won a blue ribbon for his wine at the Philadelphia Exhibition. Prohibitionists and the dour members of the Women's Christian Temperance Union weren't having any of that, so viticultural practices were pretty much buried and forgotten. It wasn't until the 1990s that an intrepid group of winemakers, recognizing that the clay- and limestone-rich soil of the county had the potential to make some of the world's best wines, started some tentative plantings again. The County Cider Company and Waupoos Estates Winery acquired winery licences, starting a trend that neither could have predicted. In 2007, the area became Ontario's newest Designated Viticultural Area under VQA legislation. The industry continued to develop quickly, and now there are some 50 vineyards and 40 thriving wineries in the county, with more coming along every year, and the region is recognized internationally for the quality of its grapes. For all of its growth, the wine industry in the county is still relatively small—some large wineries in other parts of Canada produce more wine in a year than all of the wineries in the county combined do—and the best way to discover them is just to stop by for a taste.

Winemakers, brewers, chefs, artists and entrepreneurs continue to be drawn to the county for its rich history, quality of life and sense of authenticity in numbers not seen since the days of the original Loyalists. Who knows what the next 14,000 years might bring.

TASTEMAKER PROFILE

Steve Campbell, *County Magazine*

"If you want to know about county history, you need to talk to Steve Campbell." It was a sentiment I heard time and again while researching this book. Finally, one day I just picked up the phone and called the *County Magazine*, the much loved local quarterly that Campbell has published for nearly 40 years. He answered the phone.

What is it that makes the county so appealing to so many people, I wanted to know. Why has it been rediscovered, what impact was that having on the community and how was it changing? His answers were forthright, unvarnished and candid.

"The county has always been tight as a community, even going back to settlement," he tells me. "We always counted on our neighbours to survive." Growing up on a farm on Gilead Road, he recalls that there was one combine to service all of the farms in that area. "Everybody would pool together, just like in the old threshing days of the early settlers. Eight farmers might show up at harvest time, and slowly but surely, they'd move down the road, harvesting everyone's fields. That's the kind of attitude we've always had here," Campbell notes.

It's that attitude that means people in the county will always stop and help a driver with a busted tire, or a farmer whose animals have gotten loose. "It's in our blood to be community-oriented and help out where we can," he says, "because if someone else does well, you do well."

For most of Campbell's life, the county was more or less forgotten. It was an island unto itself that major highways and politicians mostly passed by. That started to change in the past 10 years, as wave after wave of people discovered the county for the beauty of its landscape, the quality of life it offers and the sense of community that seems to be lacking for so many in the modern world.

"People don't come here because we're hip and happening," Campbell insists, "and they don't come here just because of the restaurants or wineries. They can get all that stuff in Toronto or Ottawa or Montreal. The draw here is that we have all of those things and we're two minutes away from farmland, open land, pasture land and winding country roads. You can go to an upscale restaurant in Picton or Bloomfield, and two minutes later, you can get in your car and you're alone on a country road."

He admits that there are stresses that the newcomers bring. Infrastructure sometimes struggles to keep up with the demand, and some longtime residents chafe at the influx of tourists. Nonetheless, he sees a net positive for the county and recognizes that change is necessary.

"The people I like best," he explains, "are the people who want to wander and discover. Going to the latest hot spot you read about is not that. A discovery is when you're going down a side road and you see a little A-frame sign that says, 'Art Studio.' That's a discovery. And the people who like to do that have the spirit that makes this place special."

BLOOMFIEL

WELLINGTON

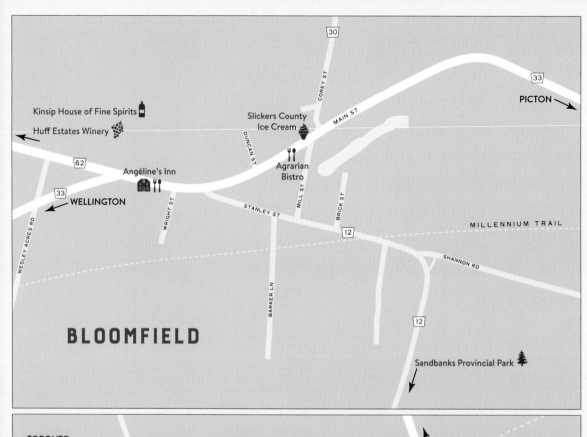

Kinsip House of Fine Spirits

Huff Estates Winery

Slickers County
Ice Cream

PICTON →

33

COREY ST

MAIN ST

62

DUNCAN ST

Angéline's Inn

Agrarian
Bistro

MILL ST

BRICK ST

33

WELLINGTON ←

WRIGHT ST

STANLEY ST

12

MILLENNIUM TRAIL

SHANNON RD

WESLEY ACRES RD

BARKER LN

12

BLOOMFIELD

Sandbanks Provincial Park

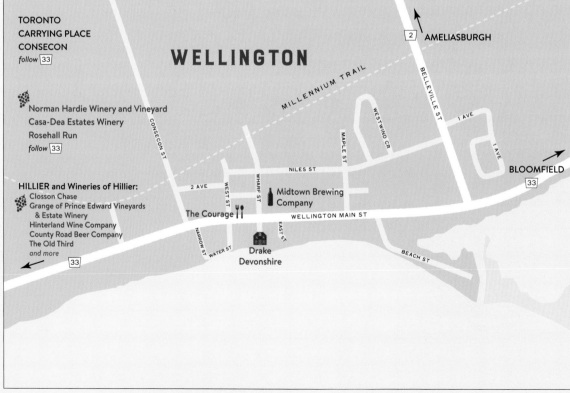

TORONTO
CARRYING PLACE
CONSECON
follow 33

WELLINGTON

2 AMELIASBURGH →

Norman Hardie Winery and Vineyard
Casa-Dea Estates Winery
Rosehall Run
follow 33

MILLENNIUM TRAIL

BELLEVILLE ST

1 AVE

CONSECON ST

WESTWIND CR

MAPLE ST

1 AVE

BLOOMFIELD →

33

NILES ST

HILLIER and Wineries of Hillier:
  Closson Chase
  Grange of Prince Edward Vineyards
    & Estate Winery
  Hinterland Wine Company
  County Road Beer Company
  The Old Third
  and more

2 AVE

WEST ST

WHARF ST

Midtown Brewing
Company

The Courage

WELLINGTON MAIN ST

EAST ST

33

NARROW ST

WATER ST

Drake
Devonshire

BEACH ST

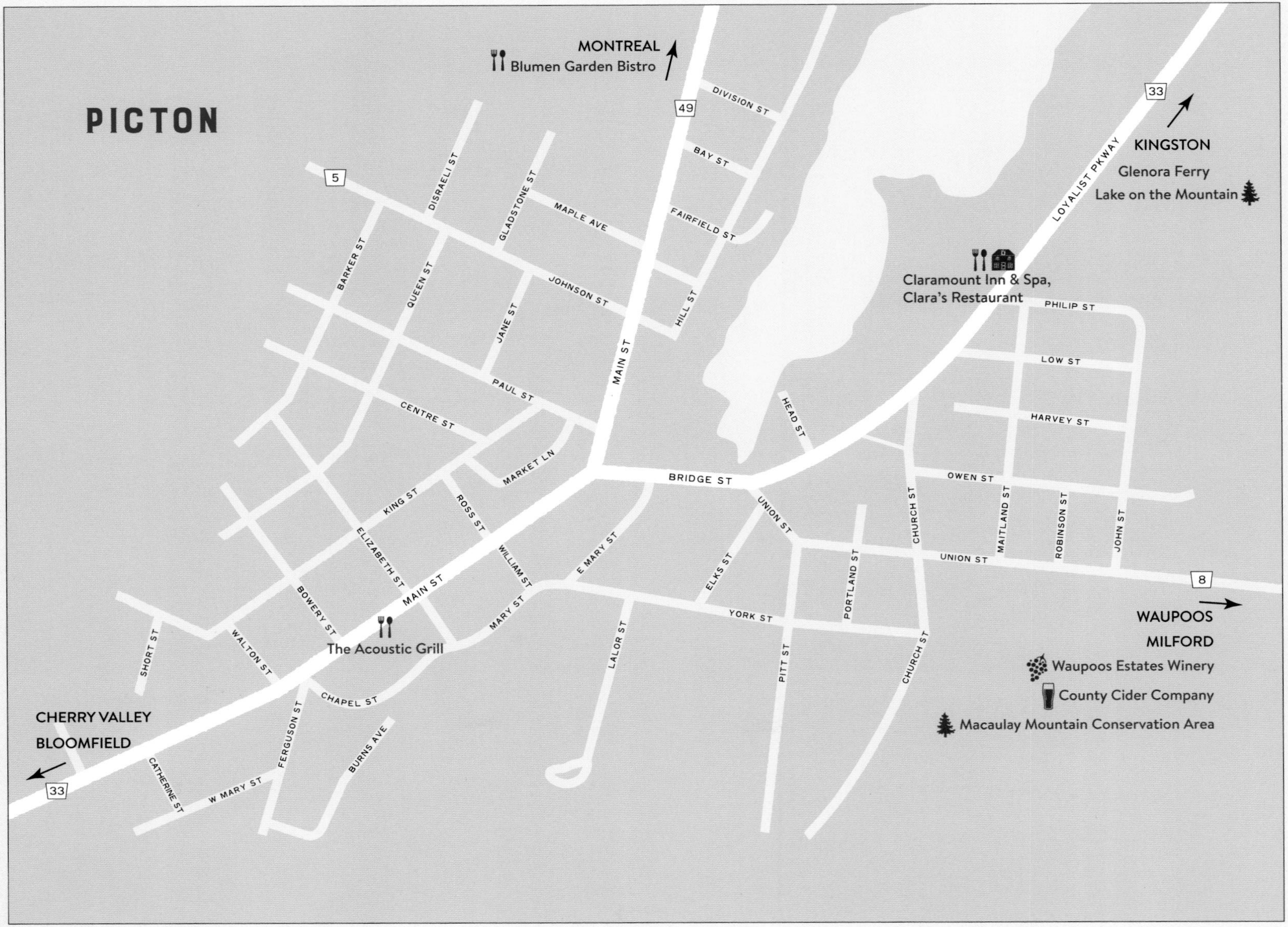

PICTON

KINGSTON
Glenora Ferry
Lake on the Mountain

[33]

MONTREAL
Blumen Garden Bistro

[49]

[5]

WAUPOOS
MILFORD

[8]

Waupoos Estates Winery
County Cider Company
Macaulay Mountain Conservation Area

Claramount Inn & Spa,
Clara's Restaurant

The Acoustic Grill

CHERRY VALLEY
BLOOMFIELD

[33]

LOYALIST PKWY

DIVISION ST
BAY ST
FAIRFIELD ST
HILL ST
PHILIP ST
LOW ST
HARVEY ST
JOHN ST
ROBINSON ST
MAITLAND ST
OWEN ST
UNION ST
CHURCH ST
CHURCH ST
PORTLAND ST
HEAD ST
UNION ST
PITT ST
YORK ST
ELKS ST
BRIDGE ST
MAIN ST
MAPLE AVE
JOHNSON ST
JANE ST
PAUL ST
MARKET LN
GLADSTONE ST
DISRAELI ST
QUEEN ST
CENTRE ST
BARKER ST
KING ST
ROSS ST
WILLIAM ST
E MARY ST
MARY ST
LALOR ST
MAIN ST
ELIZABETH ST
BOWERY ST
WALTON ST
SHORT ST
CHAPEL ST
BURNS AVE
FERGUSON ST
W MARY ST
CATHERINE ST

TASTEMAKER PROFILE

◇◇◇◇◇◇◇◇◇◇◇◇◇◇◇◇◇◇◇◇◇

Alex Fida

Second generation innkeeper, Alex Fida, is as good a concierge to the county as you'll find anywhere. For as long as he can remember, he's been scouring the back roads and backyards, checking out garage sales and hunting for treasures. Between renovating The House of Falconer, a landmark Regency cottage Fida's turning into an artists' studio, boutique hotel and personal residence; decorating and operating Angéline's Inn (Prime Minister Justin Trudeau was a recent guest); and consulting on interior design projects, he's always on the hunt for cool finds. His sharp eye and impeccable taste (Fida was recently named as one of Canada's best-dressed people) make him a great guide to all things stylish.

"The places I like to shop at are because of the people involved in them," he says. "We do a lot of work with a shop called Handworks (246 Bloomfield Main Street, Bloomfield). Just going in there is an experience. Tammy Love, the owner, is a painter and just a very creative soul—her shop is covered floor to ceiling in everything from fine handcrafts to vintage pieces. It's a unique space. It feels like an old timey hardware store, everything's everywhere, but you can ask her for something and she knows exactly where it is. It's really fun.

"In Picton, there's Kelly's Shop (197 Main Street, Picton). She's been around for over 10 years now and she has mostly women's fashion. She's a character and I think she was sort of ahead of the curve—she was one of the people who started the revival of Picton's Main Street.

"Fabric World (261 Main Street, Picton) is this old-school quilting shop. The owner is one of the most knowledgeable people you'll ever meet on the subject of quilting and has every tool you could ever need to make a quilt.

"Oak Clothing (291 Main Street, Wellington) is a new clothing shop that's hip and current. They have both men's and women's clothes and bring in labels like Cheap Monday and BB Dakota that you don't see anywhere else in the county.

"For art, I like Blizzmax Gallery near Milford. They do some interesting, semi-alternative work, and they've been around for a long time. Mad Dog Gallery also has long-standing roots, and it's so well-curated. Of course, Oeno Gallery at

Huff Estates is an important part of the local art scene, too.

"When it comes to food, I like what they're doing at the Agrarian Market. It's a specialty grocery store from the people behind the Agrarian Bistro. They've got a great selection of cheeses and charcuterie from the county and around the world. I go to Hagerman's for the sweetcorn and butter tarts. Prinzen Farms in Bloomfield has the best free-range chicken. I adore Bay Woodyard and Gavin North from Honey Pie Hives and Herbals near Cherry Valley—their honey is fantastic. Cressy Mustard Co. in Waupoos is great. And there's a wonderful honour system

market across from MacCool's Re-Use. They sell fresh herbs and medicinal herbs, but also goose eggs, which are delicious. Humble Bread, available at Wellington Farmers' Market, is also fantastic.

"For nightlife, I think the Hayloft has revived the live music scene here. It used to be a young dance place, but this new version has gone back to its original roots. It's literally a barn, with a bar and a stage, and that's it. I think they've tapped into a folksy, contemporary music scene that is really appropriate for the area."

Hotels

BLOOMFIELD

Angéline's

At last count Angéline's was, depending on how they're tallied, as many as half a dozen different properties under one brand, and still growing.

The impressive nineteenth-century main house, an Italianate beauty with fresh green shutters outside and original tin ceilings within, was once the proud home of devout Quaker preachers, later a boarding house, then grand country retreat. Now it houses five eclectic suites that combine heirloom ephemera with whimsical flourishes.

Across from the main house, the nine rooms of The Walter—formerly the Walter Motor Inn, the first motel in the county—were the height of road-trip fashion when they opened in 1950. Simple, but cleverly designed, rooms include barnboard headboards, repurposed antiques and fresh, modern bathrooms. Thanks to owner Alex Fida's sharp eye, The Walter is once again cool.

More private accommodation includes the two-storey Coach House Loft, the cozy Chalet and the impressive Babylon Log House, a mid-nineteenth-century white cedar log cabin that was disassembled at its original location 30 kilometres away and reassembled beam by beam in its new home. Offsite, in Picton, Fida also operates the 2,500-square-foot, three-bedroom Picton House and adjoining loft.

433 Main Street, Bloomfield | 613-393-3301 |www.angelines.ca

The Inn at Huff Estates

Twenty-one rooms set amid the vineyards and art-filled gardens of the sprawling Huff Estates winery. Deluxe rooms include private garden patios, while the winemaker's suite, with its floor-to-ceiling limestone fireplace, features a wraparound patio that overlooks the vineyard.

2274 County Road 1, Bloomfield | 613-393-1414 | www.huffestates.com/the-inn

Angéline's

Drake Devonshire

Away in the County

CHERRY VALLEY

Away in the County

Clever touches like an old trunk repurposed into a coffee table, a beach scene painted on a plank and salvaged hemlock repurposed into a bed frame give this sophisticated bed and breakfast its character. Three rooms—Art, Carpentry and Gardening—reflect the passion of hosts Susan and Glen Wallis. Visit Susan's encaustic painting studio and take a tour of the gardens with Glen to pick fresh produce for breakfast.

166 County Road 18, Cherry Valley |
613-476-2554 | www.awayinthecounty.com

The Black Licorice Tree

Fronterra Farm, Camp & Brewery

The June Motel

Away in the County

CONSECON

Fronterra Farm, Camp & Brewery

Summer camp for grown-ups. Here you'll find waterfront, luxury, log-framed canvas prospector tents with proper king-size beds, hot showers and private outdoor kitchens. Oh, and beer. Lots and lots of beer. The county's first organic farm brewery is currently ramping up production to start producing beer from its own farm-grown heirloom hops and malt barley. Guests can visit the farm and production facilities to get up close and personal with the beer-making process. A true "plough-to-pint" experience.

242 County Road 27, Consecon |
1-800-427-1257 | www.fronterra.ca

MILFORD

Jackson's Falls Country Inn

Innkeeper Lee Arden Lewis incorporates elements from her Mowhak heritage—fabrics, portraits, a celebrity canoe (it was used in the Johnny Depp film *Dead Man*)—with a modern aesthetic partly attached to a nineteenth-century school-house. Sounds complicated, but the result is seamless. Nine rooms plus a coach house with space to expand in a bucolic location.

1768 County Road 17, Milford | 613-476-8576 | www.jacksonsfalls.com/inn

Musicians Vera and John of Whoa Nellie performing at Jackson's Falls Inn

PICTON

Claramount Inn and Spa

Four-poster beds, freestanding tubs and Victorian antiques offer guests of this elegantly restored turn-of-the-century mansion a taste of the good life. Formerly a private home, then an apartment building and finally head-quarters for the Prince Edward Cruising Club, the inn comprises 10 rooms and suites, with three of them situated in the adjacent Carriage House. Clara's restaurant serves breakfast and dinner in a linen- and fern-bedecked space overlooking the gardens and Picton harbour. Signature treatments at the impressive Claramount Spa include a maple antioxidant wrap (utilizing local maple sugar, syrup and tea), beer pedicure (enzymes are involved) and aqua therapy in the heated saltwater pool (the county's best).

97 Bridge Street, Picton | 613-476-2709 | 1-800-679-7756 | www.claramountinn.com

Isaiah Tubbs Resort

Old-school Ontario classic camp with cottages, rooms and its own private beach. There's tennis, beach volleyball, banana boat rides and more for the adventurous, as well as sunset cruises for the rest of us.

1642 County Road 12, Picton | 613-393-2090 | www.isaiahtubbs.com

Merrill Inn

The June Motel

Every "it" destination worthy of hipster credentials has an old motel that's been refashioned into something groovy, and Picton's no different. The decidedly not happening Sportsman Motel is now the June, a bright, lively and eclectically designed (flowery wallpaper, wicker thrones, macramé wall hangings) spot where there's easy flow yoga, followed by a mimosa on Saturday mornings, and wine and doughnuts every day.

12351 Loyalist Parkway, Picton | 613-476-2424 | www.thejunemotel.com

The Manse

A vast network of patios and verandas, portes cochères and gazebos surround the impressive facade of this nearly 115-year-old landmark limestone building. Formerly a clergy house, each of the seven rooms has its own fireplace and some have private balconies. The kidney-shaped pool and hot tub are more worldly additions. Innkeeper Chris Wylie also happens to be one of the county's most talented chefs. Breakfasts are included with the room rate and while the restaurant isn't open to the public, guests can, and should, book a private meal.

10 Chapel Street, Picton | 1-877-676-1006 | www.themanse.ca

Merrill Inn

In the parlour, with comfy chairs placed just so and the flowers neatly tucked in their vases, everything's just tickety-boo. It's easy to imagine Sir John A. Macdonald sitting here discussing matters of the day with his friend, Mr. Merrill, the home's original owner. He couldn't have asked for better caretakers than innkeepers Amy and Edward Shubert, both long-time hospitality industry professionals, who purchased the historic inn back in 2002 and have set the bar for luxury in the county ever since. There are 13 rooms throughout the hotel, including the exquisite Loyalist Suite with its own wood-burning fireplace. The partnership with chef Michael Sullivan ensures a seamless blend of polished service throughout the inn and flawless food in the restaurant. Spiced pecans, Waupoos cider vinaigrette, strawberry rhubarb jam, wine jelly and the inn's own county-made amenities are available in the gift shop.

343 Main Street, Picton | 613-476-7451 | 1-866-567-5969 | www.merrillinn.com

Picton Harbour Inn

The first inn to occupy this prime location at the head of Picton Bay was opened back in the 1790s. In its current incarnation, the inn contains 29 guest rooms, as well as two apartments (one with two bedrooms, one with three), all recently updated. The Lighthouse Restaurant, a favourite with locals and open until 1.30 p.m., serves breakfast until closing time, plus solid renditions of diner classics: crisp fish and chips, an appropriately sloppy Monte Cristo and a commendable egg salad sandwich.

33 Bridge Street, Picton | 613-476-2186 | www.pictonharbourinn.com

The Royal Hotel

Once the pride of Picton, and an elegant example of a grand Victorian hotel, by the early part of this century the Royal Hotel had devolved into a seedy bar and run-down rooming house. The exterior facade was just about all that was salvageable by the time Greg Sorbara, a former Ontario finance minister, decided to revive the grand hotel's fortunes. The new 28-room hotel will bring a new level of sophistication to Main Street Picton and is a point of pride for the whole county again. (Currently scheduled to open in the fall of 2018.)

247 Main Street, Picton

The Waring House Inn and Conference Centre

With 49 rooms scattered across five buildings, The Waring House is easily the county's largest inn. A few rooms are found in the 1820s stone farmhouse that also houses Amelia's Garden restaurant and the Barley Room pub. The rest are divided among The House Next Door, The Vineyard View Cottage and the much newer Heritage and Quaker lodges, both built in 2008. Oil portraits of bonnet-clad county grandees from the distant past, delicate watercolours of local landscapes and black and white photos depicting the county's history decorate the rooms. On Sundays and Wednesdays, the inn's own cooking school guides budding chefs in the finer points of fine cooking, covering everything from building the ultimate burger to mastering sous vide cookery.

395 Sandy Hook Road, Picton | 613-476-7492 | www.waringhouse.com

Waupoos Winery Farm House

The proud, beautifully-restored brick farmhouse on the grounds of Waupoos Estates Winery offers four quaint rooms that can be booked individually or taken together as a whole. Views, especially from the upper floors, span straight across the vineyards and far into Prince Edward Bay.

3013 County Road 8, Picton | 613-476-8338 | www.waupooswinery.com/accommodations

Picton Harbour Inn

Lake on the Mountain Resort

PRINCE EDWARD

Lake on the Mountain Resort

While the seven rustic, self-catering cottages and single lakeside suite on the shores of the beautiful Lake on the Mountain are of a comparatively recent vintage, the resort's two restaurants are among the oldest structures in the county. Both The Inn and the recently restored Miller House date back to the late eighteenth century.

264 County Road 7, Prince Edward | 613-476-1321 | www.lakeonthemountain.com

|41| HOTELS

PRINCE EDWARD

Drake Devonshire

WELLINGTON

Drake Devonshire

A young couple, their hair and clothes askew, spills out of the old-timey photo booth, giggling. Nearby, two guys in beat-up ball caps—possibly local farmers, possibly visiting city hipsters—battle it out on the Ping-Pong table. Partiers on the patio watch the progress of an intense bag toss game out on the beach. Welcome to the Drake Devonshire, country cousin to renowned Toronto art space/crash pad The Drake Hotel.

Originally a foundry, then an inn and finally just a bit of an eyesore, the property dates back to the nineteenth century. The Drake's arrival in 2014 was a game changer not just for the hotel, thanks to a major refresh and update, but for the town of Wellington, which went from quaint and charming to happening and hip seemingly overnight.

With only 11 rooms and two suites, the Drake is a coveted reservation, but people who aren't spending the night still flock to the property for open-mic nights in the bar, yoga in the Glass Box, painting classes in the Pavilion or just to hang out with a drink on the deck. The Drake's country-barn-meets-camp-mess-hall-meets-modern-art-museum aesthetic apparently appeals to everyone.

24 Wharf Street, Wellington | 613-399-3338 | www.drakedevonshire.ca

ALSO NOTABLE

The Wilfrid Boutique Farmhouse

Country living complete with chickens and old barns. Guests stay in a lovingly restored 175-year-old farmhouse.

1375 Royal Road, Milford | 438-390-2505 | www.thewilfrid.com

Windhover County

Four rooms and much more, including chickens and sheep and horses! Gather honey from the hives, fresh eggs from the hens and take a pony out for a ride. Local sausage-making legend, Angelo Bean, even offers cooking classes for those who want to take their pasta game to the next level.

1109 County Road 8, Milford | www.windhovercounty.com

The Black Licorice Tree

Three-room B&B en route to Sandbanks with a pottery studio in the barn.

1287 County Road 12, Picton | 613-970-3031 | www.blacklicoricetree.com

The Wilfrid Boutique Farmhouse

Windhover County

TASTEMAKER PROFILE

◇◇◇◇◇◇◇◇◇◇◇◇◇◇◇◇◇◇◇◇

Jeff Stober

"People gravitate here for a whole host of reasons," says Jeff Stober, the entrepreneurial hotelier behind the Drake Devonshire. "I think it's fair to say there's some kind of magnetic energy that pulls people to this land."

For Stober, that energy manifested in an invitation from a friend to visit the county in 2009 to scout possible locations for a rural outpost of his popular Drake Hotel in downtown Toronto. "As soon as I saw this place I knew that it was worthy of falling head over heels for," he says. "The beautiful farmhouses, the beautiful architecture, the gorgeous village topography, that stuff you can't create. That's the magic. When you couple the history with the land, we as humans are filling in the blanks, but all of the heavy lifting or raw materials are in place."

By the time he laid eyes on the 150-year-old house with the rich history—variously an iron foundry, a nursing home and a B&B—that would eventually become the Drake Devonshire, Stober was completely won over. "The first time I saw the Devonshire it affected me deeply," he says. "I saw the potential and the fact that maybe it hadn't yet reached its full potential, so all we wanted to do was take advantage of the natural gifts that were already there."

His success in doing so was recognized far beyond the confines of the county. Almost immediately after the hotel opened in 2015, the international accolades started pouring in. Profiles in *Architectural Digest* and *The Independent* and a place on the *Condé Nast* Traveler "Hot List" meant that the hotel was quickly booked with visitors from around the world.

It continues to be to this day, but Stober demurs when asked about the impact this has had on the region. "If we opened some people's eyeballs to the beauty of the county, then we feel good about that," he says, "because it does deserve to be getting the attention that it's receiving. Other than that, we want to do a good job within our four walls and on our land and be a good neighbour and contributor to our community, which we think we're doing. Ultimately, we just want to showcase what, to our minds, is so beautiful."

Restaurants

Agrarian Bistro

BLOOMFIELD

Agrarian Bistro

Rustic barnboard and bare brick combine with snazzy chandeliers and the warm sound of vintage vinyl to give Agrarian an irresistible, easygoing appeal. As befits a restaurant inspired by all things agricultural, the menu is largely built around local ingredients, and changes with the seasons. Wild leeks with peas and ricotta might top a spring flatbread. A plump veal chop, marinated in herbaceous chermoula sauce, with hen-of-the-woods mushrooms and wilted greens could beckon in the fall, while warming pork adobo with green papaya relish brings a taste of Filipino sunshine in the winter. Sunday brunch of chicken and waffles is a can't-miss tradition for many. Downstairs, in the candlelit Speakeasy, patrons sip local craft brews at the cozy bar. Live music nights give guests an opportunity to see some of the region's best musicians in an intimate setting.

275 Bloomfield Main Street, Bloomfield | 613-393-0111 | www.agrarianpec.ca/bistro

County Road Beer Garden

HILLIER

County Road Beer Garden

In no time, County Road has grown into one of the county's must-see destinations. Even the prime minister stops by when he's in town. Packed from the time it opens until the last pint is poured, this popular little beer garden beside the Hinterland Winery is the best little bierhalle this side of Bremen. Chef Neil Dowson's seasonal menus might feature Newfoundland cold water shrimp as the star of a deconstructed shrimp cocktail one week, and a hot chicken sandwich the next. Count on fresh oysters, farmhouse cheese and charcuterie nearly every day. Growlers and mixed cases of the brewery's excellent ales, saisons and lagers are also available to bring home.

1258 Closson Road, RR1, Hillier | 613-399-5883 | www.countyrdbeer.com

Mill Pond

MILFORD

Milford Bistro

Hamlets don't come much quainter than Milford and this welcoming little bistro in the heart of "downtown"—between the library and the post office—only adds to the charm. Seasonally inspired dishes such as lake trout with poached spring vegetables, duck egg with sautéed mushrooms, and rhubarb ice cream make the most of the farm-rich location.

3048 County Road 10, Milford | 613-476-0004 | www.facebook.com/pages/Milford-Bistro /127443503961810?ref=br_rs

MILFORD

Blumen Garden Bistro

PICTON

The Acoustic Grill

Beer taps bristle around the bar like the tuning knobs on a Gretsch double-cut 12-string electric. Owners Steve Purtelle and Jenny Leigh are some of the county's biggest supporters of independent music, and few places offer a more convivial setting in which to hear it. Musicians come from far and wide to play and record here. The pub even has its own record label, Acoustic Jam Records. Though the restaurant is most famous for its burger, its potato nachos are nothing to cry the blues about either.

172 Picton Main Street, Picton | 613-476-2887 | www.theacousticgrill.ca

Amelia's Garden at The Waring House

Drawing on the bounty of over 40 local suppliers, in addition to its own substantial kitchen garden, Amelia's Garden pairs chicken liver mousse with drops of Berwick's honey, Black River cheddar with Waupoos cider, and Dewey's pickerel with artichoke risotto. That same dedication to local suppliers applies to the wine list, as well.

395 Sandy Hook Road, Picton | 613-476-7492 | www.waringhouse.com/ameliasgarden

The Acoustic Grill

Barley Room

Live music accompanies the escargots, French onion soup and smoked ribs most nights at this lively gastropub at The Waring House Inn.

13590 Loyalist Parkway, Picton | 613-476-7492 |
www.waringhouse.com/thebarleyroom

Blumen Garden Bistro

On a brisk fall day in the dining room beside the crackling fire, or in the heat of summer beneath the shade of an umbrella in the garden, chef Andreas Feller's charming little bistro never lacks for appeal. All of the modern bistro classic dishes have their charms, but for many regulars there might as well be only three dishes on the menu. To start, a shared order of Blumen's signature chickpea fries. Next, the house-pulled braised rabbit over house-made gnocchi with leeks, oyster mushrooms and lardons topped with Parmigiano-Reggiano. And for dessert? Lemon tart with lavender meringue icing and a glass of Sandbanks Estate late-harvest Vidal.

647 County Road 49, Picton | 613-476-6841 |
www.blumengardenbistro.com

Clara's

Chef Nathan Coventry likes to add surprises to classic preparations. Pecan- and herb-crusted duck breast gets part- nered with a cherry tomato and bean succotash, fennel salad gets spiked with chorizo, and winter clams are garnished with pickled herbs. Thick carpets, elaborate draperies and pressed linens make this restaurant in the Claramount Inn one of the county's most elegant.

97 Bridge Street, Picton | 613-476-2709 | www.claramountinn.com/claras-picton-dining

County Canteen

The county's original gastro pub brings many local brews and wines together to join a menu of traditional pub favourites with a few international hits thrown in. Live a little: start with the Vietnamese rice paper rolls, then have the bangers and mash. Follow a quesadilla with Khao San Road chicken wings or a Moroccan chicken Caesar wrap with a korma curry. Rules are meant to be broken.

279 Main Street West, Picton | 613-476-6663 | www.thecountycanteen.com

Merrill Inn

It was a surprise to many when chef Michael Sullivan, who had worked in some of Canada's top kitchens, decided to pack up his knives and move to the county. Now, of course, there's a veritable stampede of chefs racing to open places, but Sullivan continues to set the bar. His honest, straightforward menu includes gnudi with pine nuts, Romano cheese and fried sage leaves, rack of Ontario lamb with warm Israeli couscous and herb salad, and beef tenderloin with butter- braised leeks. And while the food might sound simple, it is built around smart ideas, expertly executed. Guests of the hotel are also advised to book one of his superb picnic baskets for a day out in the county.

343 Main Street East, Picton | 613-476-7451 | www.merrillinn.com/dine

Portabella

Local artists hang their work on the bright orange walls, fresh flowers brighten every table and gauzy curtains wave each time guests arrive. Owner Don King keeps things running smoothly, offering a warm welcome and a relaxed setting, however busy the dining room gets. The only tension is between those who insist the pan-seared pickerel with leek-vermouth cream sauce is the best dish on the menu and those who will go to the mat for the pecan chicken.

265 Picton Main Street, Picton | 613-476-7057 | www.facebook.com/portabellaonmain

The Vic Café

The Vic Café

For wholesome diners, there are wheat grass shots, turmeric-ginger smoothies and tofu rice bowls. For the hungover, there's strong coffee, scrambled eggs with thick rashers of bacon, and even a little hair of the dog in the form of Barley Days County Light beer. In the summer, the library-side patio provides some of the best people watching in Picton.

222 Main Street West, Picton | 613-476-2233 | www.theviccafe.com

County Canteen

PRINCE EDWARD

Miller House Café & Brasserie

A popular spot for international sharing platters, located across the road from the Lake on the Mountain Resort. Enjoy Iberico ham, Piave Stravecchio cheese, Black River six-year-old white cheddar, and drinks from around the world and the county in a 200-year-old house. The coveted patio seats offer dramatic views across Adolphus Reach.

275 County Road 7, Prince Edward | 613-476-1321 | www.lakeonthemountain.com/dining/the-miller -house

Waupoos Pub

An oasis of sorts for people going "around the horn" and a guaranteed good time for everyone else. The patio turns into a dance floor most Wednesday nights when there's live music and wings. The rest of the time there might be a pig roast on or a fish fry happening for fun, and there's always a great burger and imaginative poutines. If the perch taco is on as a special, have that.

2470 County Road 8, Prince Edward | 613-661-6629 | www.thewaupoospub.com

WELLINGTON

The Courage

Fire in Our Hearts, reads the neon sign on the tin wall and this feisty, new Canadian bistro, with its granite bar and custom wallpaper—made by scanning bits of flowers and finds from around the county—certainly has that. Serving breakfast (consider the breakfast poutine) and lunch (get the pumpkin chili) seven days a week and dinner (trout Wellington, of course) five nights, the Courage doesn't lack for ambition. In addition to the excellent local wine list, with plenty to choose from by the glass, there's also a good selection of "natural" wines from around the world.

298 Wellington Main Street, Wellington | 613-399-2233 | www.thecouragebar.com

Drake Devonshire

By now, brunch at the Drake is just about as much of a county tradition as a trip to Sandbanks. Avocado toast, chicken and waffles, and the gorgeous shrimp benny are already Instagram famous and taste #delicious. At lunch and dinner, the focus is on comfort: salt cod perogies, lamb rigatoni, pork schnitzel and flourless chocolate torte. The county's most sophisticated cocktail program is built around serious libations like the brown butter maple old-fashioned, pisco verde and a textbook gin and tonic.

24 Wharf Street, Wellington | 613-399-3338 | www.drakedevonshire.ca/dining

The Courage

East and Main

Dive in to seafood jambalaya, Louisiana crab cakes, and creole-rubbed Haanover View Farms pork chop with polenta and grainy mustard at this plucky little bistro on Main Street in Wellington.

270 Wellington Main Street, Wellington | 613-399-5420 | www.eastandmain.ca

Cocktails at the Drake

East and Main

ALSO NOTABLE

The Public House

The blackboards and vintage maps hint at the building's former life as a one-room schoolhouse, but the menu looks even further back for inspiration. Taking its cue from traditional aboriginal cuisine—Mohawk corn soup; Three Sisters salad with squash, corn and beans; and local fish, simply prepared—chef Meghan Van Horne is helping to bring this under-appreciated cuisine to a new audience.

1768 County Road 17, Milford | 613-476-8576 | www.jacksonsfalls.com/public-school-house

Coach's Pub & Grillhouse

Classic Canadian Pub (think: wing night Wednesdays). Live music or a DJ can be found in the back bar and there's a popular patio in the summer.

251 Main Street, Picton | 613-476-5888 | www.facebook.com/coachs-pub-grill-house -287063781313123

The Lunch Box

Like someone's dream of a school cafeteria where the tuna salad is top notch, the shepherd's pie is piping hot, and there are lemon cupcakes for dessert. Simple, unpretentious and delicious. A great place to stock up on finished dishes ahead of a picnic.

1-11 MacSteven Drive, Picton | 613-471-1222 | www.facebook.com/TheLunchBoxPEC

Pomodoro

Sand and Pearl

Bright blue raw bar, fish fry and seafood counter on the road to the Sandbanks from the people behind The Shore catering. Dishes might include octopus tostadas or snapper ceviche.

1705 County Road 12, Picton | www.sandandpearlrawbar.ca

The View Restaurant at Picton Golf & Country Club

A sort of a best-kept secret, not everyone knows that the restaurant is open to non-members and features one of the best views, overlooking Picton Bay, found anywhere in the county.

734 County Road 49, Picton | 613-476-8383 | www.pictongolf.ca/the-view-restaurant -bar-patio.php

Pomodoro

Old-school red sauce Italian classics, from fried calamari to spaghetti and meatballs with a few curve balls (jalapeño ravioli nachos, anyone?) thrown in.

280 Main Street, Wellington | 613-399-5909 | www.pomodoropec.ca

Soup Opera

French bistro classics: ratatouille, salade niçoise and escargot executed with all the care they deserve. The adjoining market sells all the ingredients the ambitious cook could need to create culinary masterpieces at home.

11 Prince Edward Drive, Wellington | 613-399-1888 | www.soupopera.ca

Sand and Pearl

TASTEMAKER PROFILE

◇◇◇◇◇◇◇◇◇◇◇◇◇◇◇◇◇◇

Cynthia Peters

A cooking class has just wrapped up at From the Farm Cooking School, but in the kitchen—an especially charming part of this elegant old 19th century farmhouse—the delicious aroma of fresh baked bread and tomato sauce still lingers. There's not a dish in sight, however; all the china is neatly lined up back in the cupboards, and the market's worth of grains, rice and pulses are all once again neatly lined up in their glass jars on the shelves.

Cynthia Peters, the owner and chef instructor who runs the place, is equally composed, despite having just tutored half a dozen novices in the finer points of pasta making. Hospitality clearly comes naturally to Peters; she ran a catering company in Toronto before moving here in 2004, and her enthusiasm for food and wine is matched only by her love of the county.

"As soon as we arrived here we knew this was the place we needed to be," she says over good espresso at her kitchen's harvest table. "For three months we came every weekend to explore the county and spend some time here. We wanted to be in an interesting and active environment. We were both food and wine lovers so that was a huge attraction, plus the arts scene and the landscape and the recreation . . . that whole combination was just irresistible."

What Peters would come to discover, however, was that beyond even the obvious attractions of the county there was an unrecognized appeal. "There's a real authenticity to this place, but it's the people in the community itself that make it so special. We didn't get to know that extra bonus of it all until we'd spent more time here. It was a winning combination for us."

Today Peters's cooking school is not just another place to learn the right way to chop an onion, it's practically a national treasure. From the Farm's full-day Culinary Adventure program is recognized as a Canadian Signature Experience, ranking up there with the Fortress of Louisbourg, Montreal International Jazz Festival and Storm Watching on Vancouver Island. "I take people to the farms," she explains, "we go to Hagerman's, sometimes we walk the fields, we go to the cheese factory, whatever we need that day. After that we have lunch and then a customized wine tour. Those are my favourite days."

Wineries, Breweries & Cideries

BLOOMFIELD

Domaine Darius

As charming as it is tiny, this adorable four-year-old winery is one of the county's youngest. The winery may be new, but winemaker Dave Gillingham has been making wines for a long time, having started out as a hobbyist in his laundry room nearly 40 years ago. That experience shows in the quality and maturity of Domaine Darius's Chardonnay, Gewürztraminer and Pinot Noir.

1316 Wilson Road, Bloomfield | 416-831-9617 | www.princeedwardcountywine.ca/wineries /domaine-darius

Huff Estates

In a region known for its ancient barns and bucolic farmhouses, the modernity of Huff Estates looks positively futuristic. When a helicopter comes chopping over the rooftops and sets down on its landing pad, that feeling is only enhanced. Owners Lanny and Catharine Huff, both county natives with deep roots in the area, built the winery as a state-of-the-art facility, focusing on high-quality, county-grown wines. They've since added a breezy restaurant and large patio where lunch is served in season. The 21-room Inn at Huff Estates offers a host of wine-inspired packages for visiting oenophiles. In partnership with the on-site Oeno Gallery, paths that lead through the four acres of gardens meander among stands of maples and poplars, flowers and herbs, all punctuated with dozens of sculptures. In addition to the 15 acres of vines that surround the winery, another 23 acres of Chardonnay, Pinot Gris, Pinot Noir, Cabernet Franc and Merlot are farmed in South Bay.

2274 County Road 1, Bloomfield | 613-393-1414 | www.huffestates.com

Huff Estates

Closson Chase

HILLIER

Broken Stone Winery

With the patio doors thrown open wide and the warm sun spilling in, it feels as if the tasting room is right in the vineyard itself. The Keupfer family—and, of course, Woody, the chocolate Lab—grows organic grapes in a way that they hope will not only produce excellent wine, but also leave the vineyard and the soil in better shape than they found it. Broken Stone is developing a reputation for quality Pinot Noir, aromatic Riesling and complex Chardonnay.

524 Closson Road, Hillier | 416-557-7565 | www.brokenstone.ca

Closson Chase

Bright purple and surrounded by flowers, the great big barn at the corner of Closson and Chase roads in Hillier is hard to miss. The wines being produced at this remarkable location are also among the county's best. Starting with an acre of test vines back in the late 80s, the vineyard has since grown to 30 acres of planted grapes and developed a reputation as a phenomenal producer of elegant, award-winning Chardonnay and sinuous Pinot Noir. Deborah Paskus is the founding winemaker and original partner along with film executives Seaton McLean and his wife, the actress Sonja Smits; Michael MacMillan

and his wife, Cathy Spoels, and others. The group is a legend in Chardonnay circles and that legacy is continued under the direction of winemaker Keith Tyers. The barn and tasting room also double as an art gallery where the work of local artists is mounted on suspended panels. See more about the winery on page 78.

629 Closson Road, Hillier | 613-399-1418 | www.clossonchase.com

Grange of Prince Edward Vineyard & Estate Winery

Mother-and-daughter winemaking wonder duo, Caroline and Maggie Granger, both grew up on this farm and know every inch of its 600 acres inside and out. A working farm for over 200 years, it's only since the turn of this century that grapes have thrived here. Today there are 60 acres, growing six varieties of grapes and all of the wine is 100-percent estate grown. Visitors can get to know the farm as well by picking up one of the popular picnic baskets, filled to the brim with local products, such as Cape Vessey and buffalo milk cheeses from Fifth Town, charcuterie from La Cultura Salumi, homemade pickles and Sprucewood cookies, and wandering out into the fields.

990 Closson Road, Hillier | 613-399-1048 | www.grangeofprinceedward.com

Gravel Hill Vineyards

Here you'll find six acres of vinifera (Cabernet Franc, Pinot Noir) and hybrid (Vidal Blanc, Seyval Blanc and Baco Noir) grapes hand-planted by owner Chris Karja and his family in the Hillier clay loam soil that this area of the county is famous for. Karja is a firm believer in the old saying that wine is made in the vineyard and his healthy, lush, lovingly tended vines clearly benefit from his attention.

567 Closson Road, Hillier | 613-399-1857 | www.gravelhillvineyards.ca

Harwood Estate Vineyards

Grapes are powered by the sun, so why shouldn't wineries be? Well, this one is. From the tasting room to the crush pad, everything is 100-percent solar powered. Eight varieties from St. Laurent to Chardonnay are planted across three vineyards, resulting in a broad portfolio of dry and off-dry reds, whites and rosés. Two dessert wines, a bright-pink blend of La Crescent and Traminette, with a bit of Frontenac Gris, and a dark, brooding, fortified port-like wine show Harwood's breadth of style.

18908 Loyalist Parkway, Hillier | 416-884-7633 | www.harwoodestatevineyards.com

TASTEMAKER PROFILE

Closson Chase & Sonja Smits

Canadian actress Sonja Smits's career has taken her from a farm in the Ottawa Valley to stages and sets around the world. It was a winery, however, that brought her and her husband, Seaton McLean, to Prince Edward County.

Closson Chase started out in 1998 as a small investment with Deborah Paskus, a vintner friend, but, like the county itself, has grown into an internationally renowned destination. Along the way, by drawing on the talents of local artisans, the winery with the purple barn has woven itself into the fabric of the community.

Take the label, for example. Created by artist David Blackwood, the painting is an interpretation of the maritime flag representing the letter C and pays tribute to the county's rich maritime tradition. Or step inside the tasting room. Stained-glass artist Vanessa Pandos created the colourful panes that surround the barn doors.

Looking across the road, you'll see the restored church that serves as housing for farmworkers. The story of that church is deeply tied to the roots of the county. "Biking from our farm to the vineyard, we'd pass by this old cemetery with a white church," Smits recalls. "Ernie Margetson, an engineer we knew, told us that his grandfather had built the church, but that it was no longer in use. The minister said, 'If you remove the church and restore the site, you can have it.' That was too good an offer, so we literally carved it up, drove it down the road and put it up at Closson Chase."

A few years later, when the roof of the church needed to be re-shingled, Smits was reminded of the architecture she and McLean had seen in Burgundy. "I spoke to Helga Boelen, a mosaic artist, and asked her to recreate the ornate tiled roof of the Hospices de Beaune."

Boelen came back with a design and Smits showed it to potential contractors, but no one wanted to do it. "Eventually, Jeff Anthony took it on. He's said he'll never do it again, but he created a work of art.

"Those kinds of relationships are important to us," Smits acknowledges, "especially because we aren't from here. There's a proud tradition of people who have been here from the Loyalists to the pioneers. That's why we named our vineyard Closson and Chase, after the farmers who established the road. You have to respect the past."

Sonja Smits

Hillier Creek Estates

Rich chords from an acoustic guitar and the smell of pizza baking in the wood-fired ovens drift across the vines, luring stragglers from the vineyard back to the 160-year-old Loyalist barn for lunch. From its 30 acres of Gamay, Pinot Noir, Chardonnay, Riesling and Vidal, Hillier produces 30,000 bottles of wine each year.

46 Stapleton Road, Hillier | 613-399-5114 | www.hilliercreekwinery.com

Hinterland Wine Company

Pioneers in a pioneering land, Vicky Samaras and her husband, Jonas Newman, were the first to produce sparkling wine in the county. Using both ancient and modern methods of wine production, Hinterland's portfolio is as diverse as it is delicious. Ancestral, their flagship wine, is made from Gamay Noir grapes using the nearly forgotten *méthode ancestrale* technique that traps the carbon dioxide created in the initial fermentation, rather than in a secondary fermentation. The result is a fun, pink wine with matching flavours of rhubarb and strawberry. Les Etoiles, by comparison an elegant and serious celebration-worthy wine, is made in the traditional way. Since releasing their first vintage back in 2007, the winery has grown by leaps and bounds. Today, the affiliated, and

adjacent, County Road Beer Company, with its bustling restaurant, is one of Hillier's most popular destinations.

1258 Closson Road, Hillier | 613-399-2903 | www.hinterlandwine.com

Lacey Estates

Kimball Lacey's winemaking roots in the county run deep. Before opening Lacey Estates, he was an assistant winemaker at Norman Hardie and an associate winemaker at Closson Chase. Those impressive credentials serve him well in his own vineyard. Opened in 2003, the family-owned winery has already gained an enviable reputation for its carefully crafted Riesling, Chardonnay, Pinot Noir and Gewürztraminer.

804 Closson Road, Hillier | 613-399-2598 | www.laceyestates.com

The Old Third

Rain falls on the roof of the impeccably renovated old hay barn, providing percussion to the piano quartet that plays over the sound system. A life-size Discobolus stands coiled beside a vintage riddling rack. On warm days, sweet and savoury crepes are served in the sunken patio, and astute listeners might hear Birdie, the vineyard's specially imported French straddle tractor, rumbling through the vineyard.

Winemaker Bruno François and his husband, Jens Korberg—a former software developer and interior designer, respectively—left city life behind in 2005 and started growing Pinot Noir and Cabernet Franc. They've since added a traditional-method sparkling apple cider made from locally grown Golden Russet apples, but have chosen to keep their portfolio tightly edited. That focus has paid off and much of the small production is eagerly snapped up as futures before it even gets to the bottle, although there's almost always a few for sale in the tasting room.

251 Closson Road, Hillier | 613-471-0471 | www.theoldthird.com

Stanners Vineyard

Pinot Noir is the main focus of winemaker Colin Stanner (his parents and wife are also hands-on in this family-owned and -run winery) with Pinot Gris and Chardonnay constituting the rest of the vineyard. The family, along with a handful of friends and a few employees, manages all seven-and-a-half acres themselves, looking after everything from weeding and canopy management to netting and harvesting. That care is apparent in the focus, clarity and terroir the wines possess.

76 Station Road, Hillier | 613-661-3361 | www.stannersvineyard.ca

Sugarbush Vineyards

So-named for the big patch of sugar maple trees in the back of the property—they make terrific maple syrup here, as well—Sugarbush calls itself the *garagiste* winery of the county. Since 2007 the winery has only made small-lot, artisanal wine from estate-grown grapes like Chardonnay, Gewürztraminer, Riesling, Viognier, Pinot Noir, Gamay and Cabernet Franc. In the winter, visitors are invited to explore the snow-shoe trails out back of the property.

1286 Wilson Road, Hillier | 613-399-9000 | www.sugarbushvineyards.ca

Trail Estate Winery

Having retired from the bakery business, owners Anton and Hildegard Sproll realized their dream of opening a winery in Prince Edward County back in 2011. Winemaker Mackenzie Brisbois, a county native, specializes in small-batch, single-vineyard wines in a wide variety of styles available exclusively at the winery or through its wine club. The winery's location, where Benway Road meets the Millennium Trail, makes it a popular spot for hikers to stop for a quick taste of unoaked Chardonnay or barrel-fermented Riesling.

416 Benway Road, Hillier | 647-233-8599 | www.trailestate.com

Traynor Family Vineyard

Back in 2008, when owner Mike Traynor first laid eyes on this plot of land at the corner of Danforth Road and Loyalist Parkway in Hillier, it was a bleak and frozen cornfield. Today it's a lush and verdant vineyard that includes the largest planting of Sauvignon Blanc in the county. In addition to that rich, almost salacious Sauvignon Blanc and a pair of hybrid reds, Traynor offers a few intriguing outliers. The Madonna Vermouth is infused with herbs and botanicals from around the winery's gardens, as well as lavender and hyssop from Prince Edward County Lavender. The winery's collaboration with Wellington's The Courage bar has resulted in three intriguing sparklers: Pét-Nat (short for *pétillant naturel*, an ancient method of making sparkling wine) Red (Marquette), White (Pinot Gris/Sauvignon Blanc) and Orange (Frontenac Gris).

1774 Danforth Road, Hillier | 1-877-403-4224 | www.traynorvineyard.com

MILFORD

Exultet Estates

Over the centuries, this prime piece of farmland in the deep south of the county has operated as an apple orchard, cheese factory and dairy farm, but it has clearly found its calling as a vineyard. Winemaker Gary Spinoza and his family bought the property in 2003 and spent a few years establishing and growing grapes for sale to other wineries. In 2008, the first vintage of Pinot Noir was produced, then Chardonnay and Vidal followed. Those three grapes still form the basis of Exultet's portfolio and that intense focus produces elegant, expressive wines with subtlety and structure. Among its many accolades, the 2011 Chardonnay was awarded the Lieutenant Governor's Award for Excellence in Ontario Wines. The Dolce Ghiacciato Vidal icewine is the only true icewine made in the county, meaning that the grapes freeze on the vine. As for the highly regarded Pinot Noir, who knows? The run is so small and the demand so high that bottles are nearly impossible to acquire.

1112 Royal Road, Milford | 613-476-1052 | www.exultet.ca

Lighthall Vineyards

Ask the winemakers in the county to name the colleagues they most respect, and Glenn Symons will appear near the top of most of those lists. From the exterior, there's nothing especially fancy about the winery, a simple Quonset hut, but there's some serious winemaking happening underneath that curved roof. Symons uses a concrete fermenting vessel, the only one of its kind in the county, for his Pinot Noir, and ages all his wines in French oak. Lighthall's Progression sparkling wine is one of the county's great bubbles. Symons recently partnered with his friend, cheesemaker Heather Robertson, and the pair now offer a selection of excellent sheep's milk cheeses.

308 Lighthall Road, Milford | 613-767-9155 | www.lighthallvineyards.com

Long Dog Winery

What started as a desire to have a place to get away to on the weekends has grown into a full-fledged winery. Sitting on 300 acres of limestone soil just outside of Milford will do that to you. Named for their love of long-haired dachshunds, the winery produces three styles of Pinot Noir, two of Chardonnay and extremely limited amounts of Pinot Gris and Rosé. The ultimate goal, however, is simply to make "the best Pinot Noir in the world."

104 Brewers Road, Milford | 613-476-4140 | www.longdog.ca

PICTON

County Cider Company

In the fall, when the apples hang on the trees like ornaments—crimson Northern Spy, golden green Michelin, bright Ida Red—and the surrounding forest is a riot of colourful leaves, there may be no more beautiful spot on earth than right here. It is pretty gorgeous in the summer, too, when the flower-filled patio is busy with visitors and the wood-fired oven is turning out crisp pizzas.

The Howes family has been growing apples on this exceptional plot of land, with a clear view across the orchard to Waupoos Island and Prince Edward Bay in the distance, for more than 150 years, and making cider for more than 20. A pair of restored limestone barns serve as the tasting room and restaurant, and it is that same limestone soil that imparts such a distinct crispness to the ciders.

657 Bongards Crossroad, Picton | 613-476-1022 | www.countycider.com

Del-Gatto Estates

Fourth-generation winemaker Pat Del-Gatto brings to bear the lessons and skills handed down from his great-grandfather, grandfather and father on the cold-climate grapes of Prince Edward County. Some of the challenges are a little different from those his forebears dealt with in Southern Italy, but the result is still great wine. Del-Gatto specializes in hybrid grapes like Seyval Blanc, St. Croix, Frontenac Noir and Vidal Blanc as well as vinifera. A little taste of Italy in Ontario.

3609 County Road 8, Picton | 613-476-8198 | www.del-gattoestates.ca

Devil's Wishbone

The first European settlers to this area, up near Lake on the Mountain, a few kilometres northeast of Picton, nick-named it the Devil's Wishbone because the soil was so poor and the land so difficult to farm. Nonetheless, a little microclimate up here, on an escarpment 100 metres above Adolphus Reach, provides enough additional heat to bring richness to the wines.

After a tour of the century barn that serves as a tasting room, pick a patio over-looking the vineyards or Adolphus Reach and taste through the entire portfolio. There are only three wines: a well-structured Riesling, a black cherry-redolent Pinot Noir and a lush Cabernet Franc.

1014 County Road 7 RR4, Picton | 613-476-1199 | www.devilswishbone.com

Half Moon Bay Winery

At the south end of Prince Edward Bay lies Half Moon Bay, a location as lovely as its name. The winery occupies a ridge overlooking the water where Pinots—Noir and Gris—Chardonnay, Riesling and Merlot soak up the sun and the view and are all grown without synthetic pesticides or fertilizers.

3271 County Road 13 RR3, Picton | 613-476-4785 | www.hmbwinery.ca

Three Dog Winery

Come for the wines, stay for the golden retrievers. Or vice versa. Either way, the bright orange and blue winery near the eastern edge of the county always offers a warm welcome. In the great tradition of pioneering county winemakers, John and Sacha Squair spent the first years coming up on the weekends and sleeping in a tent on their land while planting grapes by hand. Pinots Noir and Pinot Gris were the first vines planted back in 2000 and slowly but surely the couple has added vines and varietals until today they offer a carefully curated selection that includes two styles of Riesling (dry and off-dry), a Baco Noir, a rosé and a few proprietary blends.

1920 Fish Lake Road, Picton | 613-403-4323 | www.threedogwine.com

Waupoos Estates Winery

To hear Ed Neuser and Rita Kaimins, founders of Prince Edward County's first modern winery, tell it, there was no master plan: no soil inspections, no complex volume production evaluations, no vision board. They just went for it. After a few glasses of wine. On a lark.

That first half-acre of vines, planted back in 1993, led to a few more and a few more, until fully 20 acres of the estate's more than 100 acres of lakefront property were planted with a dozen varieties of red and white grapes. In 2012, the winery was sold to the Donini family (best known as the producers of Donini Chocolate) and since then the estate has grown as much as the vineyard and now almost operates as its own little community within a community. All summer, the peaked white tent pavilion, set among the lush vineyards, is busy with wedding parties. The vast, octagonal Gazebo Restaurant largely draws on its own garden for produce. Baby bunnies, pot-bellied piglets and bouncy lambs vie to outdo each other in cuteness over at the petting zoo (yes, there's a petting zoo). The Clafeld Fruit Winery Market and Cider House is a grocery store in miniature and the recently added Chocolatier and Candy Store—there's also terrific gelato—ensure that no indulgence goes unfulfilled.

3016 County Road 8, Picton | 613-476-8338 | www.waupooswinery.com

PRINCE EDWARD

Black Prince Winery

There just aren't that many places in the world where wine grapes and the kind of oak trees suitable for making barrels grow together. In Prince Edward County they do, so when winemaker Geoff Webb met barrel-maker Pete Bradford, the two knew they were on to something. Both the Terroir Elite Chardonnay and Knight's Quest Pinot Noir are aged in barrels made right on the property, as are the variety of oak-aged vinegars (single varietal red wine, fruit and even hemp vinegars).

13370 Loyalist Parkway, Prince Edward | 613-476-4888 | www.blackprincewinery.com

Cape Vineyards

The vines date back to the 1990s, but were in pretty rough shape when Michael Lewis bought the property in 2010. By 2013, he and his county-born and -raised wife, Kristen Rogers, had returned the vineyard to life and completed construction of their winery. Today, Cape Vineyards produces wine exclusively from estate-grown grapes: dark, intense Merlot and Cabernet Franc, buttery Chardonnay and crisp Riesling.

4203 County Road 8 RR4, Prince Edward | 613-476-7770 | www.capevineyards.ca

WELLINGTON

By Chadsey's Cairns

This historic, 200-year-old farm, originally owned by early settler Ira Chadsey, comprises more than 141 acres—including a set of antique stone cairns (hence the name)—with 14 acres dedicated to vines. The tasting room—a former apple barn—dates back to the mid-nineteenth century. Best known for their Chenin Blanc and Chardonnay, BCC is also one of the county's premier rosé (both still and sparkling) producers.

17432 Loyalist Parkway, Wellington | 613-399-2992 | www.bychadseyscairns.com

Casa-Dea Estates Winery

A proud member of the great trio of wineries on Greer Road, Casa-Dea is by far the largest. 65 acres of vineyard planted with Cabernet Franc, Riesling, Gamay, Chardonnay and Pinot Grigio, the wines are a love letter to founder Domenic Di Pietrantonio's Italian heritage and his wife, for whom the winery is named. The winery's La Pergola restaurant serves delicious versions of Italian classics: bruschetta, penne à la vodka, tiramisu. Work off lunch with a bocce match or book out the guest house and make a weekend of it.

1186 Greer Road, Wellington | 613-399-3939 | www.casadeaestates.com

Karlo Estates

Barn cats slink between the feet of guests in the wine lounge and birds nest in the rafters of the sprawling old barn that is the heart of this charming winery. Bottles for sale in the tasting room are stored in antique tomato crates, as an homage to the farm that thrived here for 250 years. They call Karlo the best little port house in the county, because of its commitment to fortified wine, but there are currently 27 different styles in the estate's portfolio. As this is the world's first vegan winery, none of the wines, from the freshest Pinot Gris to the most contemplative blend, utilize any animal products (egg whites, isinglass, gelatin) during the winemaking process. The winery's dry-stone bridge, a popular spot for vegan picnickers, is the largest in North America.

561 Danforth Road, Wellington | 613-399-3000 | www.karloestates.com

Keint-He Winery and Vineyards

Old-world style wines from one of the world's newest wine regions. Taking full advantage of the limestone soil the grapes thrive in to produce classic, character-driven Pinot Noir, Chardonnay, as well as small amounts of Riesling and Gewürztraminer. There's often live music al-fresco on the weekends and the patio overlooks the sweep of Lake

Ontario. Unique to the county, the winery's "movie in the vineyard" nights have included screenings of *Planes, Trains and Automobiles* and *The Big Lebowski*, BYO White Russian.

49 Hubbs Creek Road, Wellington | 613-399-5308 | www.keint-he.ca

Norman Hardie

The long driveway to Norman Hardie's is flanked by vines. As the car descends the hill toward the winery, clay and limestone, part of an ancient seabed and a key component of these wines, crackle under the tires. The winery itself, a long, red barn with a distinct tin roof, is always active with workers bustling back and forth. Guests on the stone patio, shaded by umbrellas, take a decidedly more relaxed approach, raising their glasses to toast one another over crisp, wood-fired pizzas and big plates of fresh greens. It's not uncommon for visitors to spend their whole day here.

As much fun as there is to be had on the patio, there's serious wine to consider upstairs in the tasting room. Hardie focuses primarily on Pinot Noir and Chardonnay, but makes smaller batches of many different cool-climate varietals like Riesling, Pinot Gris and Cabernet Franc. His Calcaire—a blend of Chardonnay, Pinot Gris and Riesling named for the limestone that gives the wine its minerality—is especially prized. Globally renowned for their finesse, fruit expression and sense of terroir—that ineffable quality that is a combination of climate, soil and topography—Hardie's wines are among the best Canada has ever produced. See more about Hardie on page 96.

1152 Greer Road, Wellington | 613-399-5297 | www.normanhardie.com

Rosehall Run

Every year since 2001, when owners Dan and Lynn Sullivan and their brother-in-law Cam Reston first planted grapes on this 150-acre property, has brought changes: first a small barn to make wine, then a small tasting bar, followed by a modern winery and new barrel room. Sullivan's wines—he's best known for Pinot Noir and Chardonnay—are some of the most highly decorated in the county. An updated tasting room came along in 2011 and for the past few summers the excellent PicnicPEC food truck has set up shop just beside the tasting room. The fried chicken sandwich is a county classic.

1243 Greer Road, Wellington | 613-399-1183 | www.rosehallrun.com

Sandbanks Winery

The lawn is punctuated with a rainbow of colourful Muskoka chairs, and more beckon from the shade of the vast, covered porch, while a few picnickers have taken advantage of the tables set up right on the edge of the vines. Sandbanks Winery, like Sandbanks itself, is all about fun. Light and refreshing wines like their Shoreline Chardonnay, Pinot Noir rosé and cheekily named French Kiss are built for sipping in the sun.

17598 Loyalist Parkway, Wellington | 613-399-1839 | www.sandbankswinery.com

TASTEMAKER PROFILE

◇◇◇◇◇◇◇◇◇◇◇◇◇◇◇◇◇◇◇

Norman Hardie

There's only one Canadian wine available by the glass in the luxurious bar of the Four Seasons in Tokyo: Norman Hardie's Pinot Noir. It is the same wine that the prime minister served to Barack Obama. The same wine that Prince Charles and Camilla tasted from the barrel when they visited the winery. The same wine, along with his luscious Chardonnay, that oenophiles around the world consider to be some of the best Canada has ever produced.

Born in South Africa and raised in Botswana, Hardie, after years working as a sommelier, decided to pursue winemaking in earnest and trained with some of the top producers in Burgundy, Oregon, California and South Africa. He could have applied those skills to produce wine anywhere, but he couldn't resist the limestone soil of Prince Edward County.

"Back in 2000, I'd tasted some wines out of Niagara," he recalls. "They had character and great potential, so I started tasting more. I got quite excited about Niagara and started looking at properties. Before I bought, though, someone told me to look in Prince Edward County.

"I got off the highway, looked at the soil and thought, 'Holy smokes, this is young, fractured limestone. This is amazing, but what's the catch?' Another vintner explained it. The catch is minus-25-degree weather. There's no ifs, ands or buts—it kills vines. In those days, winemakers were hilling up [burying the vines in the earth to protect them from frigid temperatures], but the techniques were primitive. Still, I loved the soil, so I found a property for sale."

Today, the winery-side patio at his 25-acre property in Hillier is the first stop for many arriving in the county, whether it's their first visit or their fiftieth. The winery has grown from producing 6,000 cases of its first vintage to more than a quarter million cases now. Hardie, when he isn't travelling the world to promote his wines to new markets, is often on hand, greeting guests, delivering pizza from the wood-fired oven and joining friends for a taste of the latest vintage.

It is idyllic now in the heart of summer, and though Hardie knows that winter is just around the corner and spring is always treacherous, he's unfazed. "The great wines have always been made on the edge," he says, "and this is definitely the edge."

HRH Prince Charles
and Norman Hardie

COUNTY BREWS

They are lined up five deep: women in wide-brimmed hats, fellas in plaid and sneakers—and vice versa—waiting to get a taste of **County Road Beer Company**'s latest batch. It seems like owner Jonas Newman is in six places at once, welcoming guests, filling up growlers, dropping off plates of flank steak with wild garlic chimichurri, and spicy merguez sausage with hummus, explaining the flavour profile of a cherry gose—"coriander, a bit of taffy."

It will continue like this throughout the weekend. No sooner is a table cleared than a new batch of guests—old friends and first-time visitors—fills it.

One hundred and fifty years ago, long before grape growers discovered the limestone-rich soils were also beautifully suited to vinifera grapes, the county was renowned for growing some of the best hops and barley in North America. Most of it was shipped off to breweries in New York and turned into beer. A trade tariff put an end to the original barley days and the county's love affair with beer all but evaporated.

It wasn't until 2007, when **Barley Days Brewery** (www.barleydaysbrewery.com) opened, that commercial beer brewing returned to the island. Appropriately, many of brews Barley Days crafts pay tribute to county history. Loyalist Lager, a crisp, golden Pilsner-style lager, is worthy of Lieutenant Archibald MacDonnell— leader of the first Loyalist settlers—himself. Royal George Brown Ale, malty and caramelized, is as sharp and elegant as the 12-gun British corvette it's named after. Sugar Shack Ale, a light, subtly sweet amber ale, is made with maple syrup tapped right in the county.

Lake on the Mountain Resort also began brewing in 2007 with a small onsite brewery featuring two styles that were only available to guests of the restaurants at the resort. Over the years the popularity of the beer grew, though, and in 2016 they moved the brewing facility down the road to Glenora and opened **Lake on the Mountain Brewery** (www.lakeonthemountainbrewco.com), a bottle shop with a beer garden and tap room. Hops grow next door and make their way into some of the batches.

Opened in 2015, Picton's **County Canteen** (www.thecountycanteen.com), holds the honour of being the first brew pub in the county. The response was so overwhelming that owners Nat and Drew Wollenberg quickly realized they needed to expand. Two years later, **555 Brewing** (www.facebook.com/555brewingco) opened just down the road and once again the Wollenbergs have found themselves with something of a hot spot on their hands. The wood-fired oven turns out pizza at a furious pace, but the expanded brewing facilities mean that there's plenty of Watermelon Kettle Sour, The Jury IPA and coffee-infused Long Black to go around.

The old blacksmith's shop in Bloomfield sat unloved and borderline uninhabitable for years before Chris and Samantha Parsons found it. The couple spent months taking the building apart and reassembling it at their property as the tap room for their highly regarded **Parsons Brewing Company** (www.parsonsbrewing.com). While their flagship, Crushable Pilsner, is a straight-forward, easy-drinking unfiltered summer-time beer, they also aren't afraid to dabble in esoterica. Letitia's Lust, a mixed saison and ale yeast concoction, is named after Letitia Youmans, a notorious local leader of the temperance movement in the county in the nineteenth century. Mestizo combines county barley with varieties grown in Patagonia while the Devil's Right Hand is barrel-aged in Wild Oak Whiskey Barrels from Kinsip House of Fine Spirits.

"We're kind of surf inspired," says surfer Aaron McKinney, owner of the new **Prince Eddy's Brewing Company** (www.princeeddys.com). "Really, we're just trying to make the ultimate beach beer." Housed in what used to be a plumbing warehouse in Picton's industrial area, the brewery is a glistening, new, steel-lined space with a mezzanine-level tasting room overlooking the whole brewing process. Flagship beers include a crisp Chin Dropper Blonde Ale and Fresh

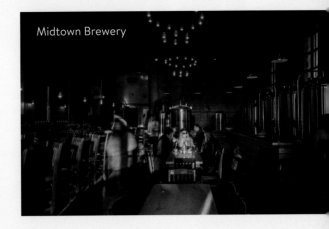

Midtown Brewery

Coast IPA, while seasonal beers utilize Barn Owl Malt, from Belleville, and the county's own Pleasant Valley hops.

"Our whole focus is flavour and the traditional classic styles. I want to make only what we think is the best representation of each beer or ale style," says "Spike" Lees, head brewer and self-described chief bottle washer at **Midtown Brewing Company** (www.midtownbrewingcompany.com) Lee, along with partner, Mark Andrewsky, spent two years turning the old meat packing warehouse just off Wellington's main street into their new brewery, restaurant and grocery store. There's a lot going on, but beer remains the focus. The traditional ESB (extra special bitter) balances malt and hops, resulting in a dry chocolate flavour upfront and caramel notes, which lead to a clean finish. Other classics include a dark Irish stout and a very peachy German kölsch. The Belgian Triple is made with local honey and maple syrup before being aged for a year.

ALSO NOTABLE

Kinsip House of Fine Spirits

Proving that the county is about more than just wine, beer and cider. Small batch spirits from vodka and gin to rye and rum. The oak-aged Black Dragon Shochu gives a county spin to Korea's most popular spirit.

66 Gilead Road, Bloomfield | 613-393-1890 | www.kinsip.ca

Redtail Vineyard

By utilizing a combination of solar power and thermal energy, Redtail can truly claim to be Canada's first off-grid, green winery. Grapes have been off-grid since the beginning of time, of course, but even they seem to appreciate the effort. With a focus on Burgundian style Pinot Noir, Gamay, Pinot Gris and Chardonnay—and a bit of Riesling thrown in for good measure—this young vineyard has already established itself as one to watch in the county.

422 Partridge Hollow Road, Consecon | 613-965-0893 | www.redtailvineyard.com

The Old Third

Attractions

NATURAL   107

MAN-MADE   127

AMELIASBURGH

Harry Smith Conservation Area

Turtles, geese and blackbirds are the main inhabitants now but, at one time, this tranquil area on the edge of Ameliasburgh was a bustling centre of industry. Roblin's Mill, a large grist mill built in 1842, operated day and night turning out 100 barrels of flour a day for nearly 80 years. In 1960 the mill was removed and rebuilt at the Black Creek Pioneer Village in Toronto, but the area remains a lovely place to spend an afternoon. The nearby Grove Cemetery is where Prince Edward County's unofficial poet laureate, Al Purdy, is buried.

Purdy Street, Ameliasburgh | 613-968-3434

CARRYING PLACE

The Millennium Trail

The chorus of birds and the buzzing of cicadas are just about the only constant on this 49-kilometre trail built on an abandoned Canadian Pacific Rail line that crosses the county. The landscape shifts from marsh to vineyard, farmland to village, and along the way deer and rabbits, beavers and turtles mingle with all manner of birdlife, from meadowlarks to mergansers, and 200 species more. A favourite with hikers and cyclists in the summer, in winter the trail becomes a magnet for Nordic skiers.

Access points in Carrying Place, Consecon, Wellington, Bloomfield and Picton

Sandbanks Provincial Park

CONSECON

North Beach Provincial Park

This slender ribbon of sand that divides North Bay from Lake Ontario is basically Sandbanks in miniature. The sand is soft and the swimming is fine, while the crowds tend to be somewhat less thick. There's also great fishing for bass, pike and perch to be had.

440 North Beach Road, Consecon | 613-393-3319

MILFORD

Point Petre Wildlife Conservation Area

Hunt for fossils along the shore edge, explore the headlands and bays in the shallow water, or wander inland among the dogwoods and cedars to discover the wetlands. Situated at the southernmost tip of the county, the waters around here are filled with shipwrecks and sunken aircraft. The lighthouse on the grounds of the meteorological research station is a replacement for the original 19-metre-high tower that was built here in 1833. Impress the locals by correctly pro-nouncing "Petre" as "Peter."

Entrance at the intersection of County Road 24 and Army Reserve Road

Prince Edward Point National Wildlife Area

Few birds have a call as ecstatic as the bobolink. Its distinct, gleeful song stands out even against the mighty yellow-rumped warbler, the narcissistic eastern whippoorwill and the rose-breasted grosbeak, all of which, along with more than 300 other species, pass noisily through this important birding area. The Prince Edward Point Bird Observatory, a Canadian Migration Monitoring Network Station, is situated within the wildlife area and is open in spring and fall. The 518-hectare site includes a wide range of habitats, from pristine beaches to grassland, limestone cliffs to forest.

Long Point Road, Milford | 1-800-668-6767

PICTON

H. J. McFarland Conservation Area

Named for the renowned philanthropist and former mayor of Picton whose wife graciously donated the seven acres of waterfront land, this popular picnic spot affords stunning views over Picton Bay.

McFarland Park Lane, Picton | 613-968-3434

Lake on the Mountain

Nobody seems to know for sure the source of the constant flow of exceptionally clean, fresh, clear water that keeps Lake on the Mountain full. Long considered bottomless, the depth of this mysterious lake, set 60 metres above Adolphus Reach, is still unknown.

296 County Road 7, Picton | 613-393-3319

Macaulay Mountain Conservation Area

Strawberry Fields, The Labyrinth, Slushbuggy Run, Groovy Tuesday: the names of some of the cycling trails that wind through these 178 hectares are as mind-bending as the scenery. In addition to these seriously challenging mountain biking trails, there are plenty of meandering walks and peaceful places to sit and ponder the view. Not all of the attractions are of the natural variety, though. Birdhouse City features more than 100 miniature reproductions of notable local buildings including a lighthouse, drugstore and even a McDonald's. The grandest birdhouse of them all is an 80-room, metre-square replica of the Massassauga Park Hotel.

224 County Road 8, Picton | 613-354-3312

PRINCE EDWARD

Little Bluff Conservation Area

Easy to miss, hard to forget. The 20-metre-high limestone bluffs provide a dramatic perch overlooking Prince Edward Bay. The pebbly barrier beach at the base of the cliffs offers some of the best skipping stones in the county and protects a rich wetland that's home to lots of great blue herons, Canada geese and bitterns. This was once an important stop for the schooners that hauled hops and barley from here in the mid- to late nineteenth century, so keep an eye out for the remains of one of the old grain storage facilities. Oh, and don't worry about the water snakes, they're more afraid of you than you are of them, and are better at swimming anyway.

County Road 13 and Whattams Road, Prince Edward

Massassauga Point

Once home to the Massassauga Park Hotel—a real hot spot in the late nineteenth and early twentieth centuries—steamers would regularly deposit crowds on these shores. People came for the dancing, croquet, leap frog (it was a simpler time) and the mineral baths. The Great Depression put an end to all that, though, and the original hotel was

scrapped for lumber in the 1950s. The foundation and a walkway to the beach are all that remain. Today the long shoreline includes both sand and cobblestone beaches, and in the winter there are some excellent cross-country ski trails.

Massassauga Road, Prince Edward | 613 968-3434

Sandbanks Provincial Park

Sun worshippers loll on the soft sand, children splash in the shallow surf and kite surfers catch air off the big rollers further out. Trails wind through the dunes, 500 campsites offer comfortable places to spend the night and canoes are quietly paddled along the Outlet River.

Formed by the world's largest bay-mouth barrier dune formation, Sandbanks has been the county's premier tourist attraction for more than 150 years. Spanning 1,600 hectares, the park attracts nearly half a million human visitors each year, more than 200 species of birds and countless wildflowers. The Friends of Sandbanks, a non-profit charitable group dedicated to the preservation of the park, has published *Sandscapes*, an excellent overview of the history, geology and ecology of the area.

3004 County Road 12, Picton | 613-393-3319

Wellers Bay National Wildlife Area

The islands, sand spits and beaches of this 83-hectare wildlife area are home to a wide range of species, from sparrows and scoters to monarch butterflies and rare hog-nosed snakes. Formerly it was a weapons range for National Defence, so access to the area requires a permit that can be acquired by contacting the Environment and Climate Change Canada regional office:

4905 Dufferin Street, Toronto | 1-800-668-6767 (in Canada only) | ec.enviroinfo.ec@canada.ca.

Bay of Quinte

WAUPOOS

Rutherford-Stevens Lookout
Little more than a picnic table and a wide viewing stand, the real draw here is the view across Smith's Bay and Waupoos Island to Point Traverse. In autumn, the vista looks like something out of a Group of Seven painting.

County Road 13 between Waupoos and Black River | 613-968-3434

WELLINGTON

Wellington Rotary Public Beach

While the Outlet Beach at Sandbanks will always be the one most closely associated with the county, this stretch of white sand, just a few flip-flopped steps from the restaurants and cafés of Wellington, has its own set of charms. In addition to the usual shore-side pursuits of tanning, swimming and picnics, the long boardwalk is interspersed with interpretive signs that reveal interesting facts about the history, botany, wildlife and geography of the area.

Beach Street, Wellington | 613-966-5500

Wellington Lighthouse

TASTEMAKER PROFILE

◇◇◇◇◇◇◇◇◇◇◇◇◇◇◇◇◇◇◇◇◇

Terry Sprague

From bald eagles to bobolinks, and meadowlarks to warblers, the bird life in Prince Edward County is among the most diverse and dramatic in all of Canada. At present, there are 357 species identified that have passed through at one time or another, and naturalist Terry Sprague has seen them all. For 50 years, Sprague wrote the nature column in *The Picton Gazette*. His interest in birds led him to look more closely at natural history in general, and his columns have covered everything from the state of the bald eagle population in the county to reports of opossum sightings and what that meant for the local environment.

With a white-throated sparrow singing its distinctive song in the background—"Pure sweet Canada, Canada, Canada"—I spoke with Sprague about what makes birding in the county so special.

For Sprague, the best time of year is in the spring when hundreds of species migrate north across Lake Ontario and

Lake Erie from their winter feeding grounds back to the boreal forests. For many birds, Prince Edward Point is the first piece of land they see after crossing Lake Ontario and, exhausted, hungry and in need of a rest, they'll settle down there in great numbers.

"It's just a delightful time of the year," Sprague says. "The males are in bright breeding plumage and they're in full song. It's quite a treat to be there when that's happening."

The first to arrive are the killdeer, "although, there's been many a snow fall after the killdeer arrive," Sprague is quick to point out. "As March goes into April, you're getting white-throated sparrows and brown thrashers, and mockingbirds and white-crowned sparrows won't be far behind. The warblers—I particularly love the warblers—are the culmination of the migration in May, and come June everything slows right down. In the fall, it starts all over again, though, with the birds going south."

After all these years, Sprague is still amazed by the diversity of the bird life and the thrill of the unexpected that each year brings. Vagrants, as naturalists call birds that show up outside of their normal migratory routes, keep things exciting. One year it might be a black-bellied whistling duck, a bird that normally doesn't come further north than Texas, or a neotropical cave swallow.

"One that keeps coming along is called a chuck-will's-widow," he says, "which is sort of a southern version of the familiar whippoorwill. One seems to appear every year in the Milford area, just singing its own little particular song."

It's hard not to be charmed by thought of this little nocturnal nightjar travelling all the way up from the deep south to spend summers in Prince Edward County. Sprague's delight in the little bird makes it seem like there must be no better way to spend your days than looking and listening for these visitors. "That's what I like about it," he says, "not just about birding, but about natural history in general. You're learning something every day."

Bloomfield Town Hall

Dead People's Stuff

ANTIQUES
BLOOMFIELD

Dead People's Stuff

To be fair, some living people's stuff does occasionally find its way into the eclectic mix of furniture, glassware, doors and whatnots, but by and large, this converted garage remains true to its name.

388 Bloomfield Main Street, Bloomfield | 613-393-3193 | www.deadpeoplesstuff.ca

BLOOMFIELD

CONSECON

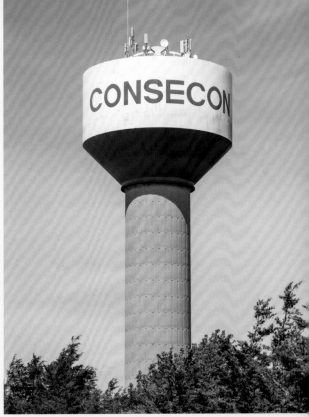

The Sword

Flintlocks and muskets, bayonets and two-handed swords, basically everything the well-dressed fireplace mantle needs. Military paraphernalia is offset by antique jewellery and a collection of the highly sought after Blue Mountain Pottery pieces.

20581 Loyalist Parkway, Consecon |
613-392-2143 | www.swordantiques.ca

The millpond in Consecon

PICTON

Frugal & Company

Filled to the rafters with all of the things you didn't know you needed: a vintage Chinese checkers board game, the original Partridge Family album in vinyl, a rusty bucket emblazoned with the words "Pure Ontario Honey." Somehow, this seemingly random collection of retro farmhouse knick-knacks and repurposed bagatelles, gathered together under one roof on Picton's main drag, all seems to fit together.

167 Main Street, Picton | 613-476-5151 | www.frugalandcompany.com

MacCool's Re-Use

Hutches from the 50s, string art from the 60s, green shaded lamps from the 70s, harvest tables that might be one or one hundred years old, all stuffed into a ramshackle 150-year-old barn. Cindy MacCool sources the majority of the antiques, while her husband, Colm, a sculptor and designer, repurposes salvaged materials into fresh new pieces and creates custom pieces from scratch.

1149 County Road 12 (West Lake Road), RR1, Picton | 613-393-5797 | www.maccoolsreuse.com

Kokito

COUNTY SHOPS BLOOMFIELD

Cannery Row

Bringing style and heritage together, sisters Jane Rutters and Susan Felton combine their love of county history with an artistic sensibility to create unique furnishings and home accessories. Benches covered in material that reproduces pages from old county newsprint; dishtowels; mugs; postcards with vintage canning label art, land deeds and old maps; and wooden puzzle maps give these fragments of history a new lease on life.

287 Main Street, Bloomfield | 613-393-3330 | www.canneryrowpec.ca

Green Gables Gifts and Greetings

Pick a holiday, any holiday—Tet, Diwali, Eid al-Fitr—chances are there's something to mark the occasion at this jam-packed (yes, they have jam, and backpacks and musical instruments and stuffed animals and scented candles) beautiful, brick Victorian on Main Street in Bloomfield.

286 Main Street, Bloomfield | 613-393-1494 | www.greengablesbloomfield.com

Kokito

With its wood-turned spurtles (a.k.a. Scottish porridge stirrers, natch) and candle holders, campfire roasting sticks and tiger lily seed packs, this isn't so much a shop as an illustrated guide to better living. That good old Canadian cottage country aesthetic has never looked so chic.

285 Main Street, Bloomfield | 613-393-2828 | www.kokito.ca

Sand and Sumac

Kokito's sister shop is directly across the street and continues the impeccably stylish theme with more of an emphasis on Moroccan silk kilims, local art, ceramics, jewellery and blankets.

288 Main Street, Bloomfield | 613-393-2828 | www.kokito.ca

CONSECON

Walt's Sugar Shack

Each year, when the first hints of spring whisper through the maples and the sweet smells of smoke and sap fill the air around Consecon, locals know it's syrup season. What started out as a simple DIY project—40 trees tapped by hand—has grown over the years to a state-of-the-art facility with 1,200 taps in production. Vintage farm implements such as saws, threshers, rakes and what-even-is-thats line the walls and ceiling of the county's most famous shack. Karen and Brian are the fourth generation of the Walt family to work this land and while they're busiest during syrup season, there always seems to be a shindig, BBQ, pancake breakfast or some other event happening at this lively farm. Sweet gift baskets, handmade quilts and all manner of maple products from syrup and butter to toffee and cotton candy fill the bustling gift shop. As suits a more than 100-year-old farm, there are plenty of other products besides maple syrup. Walt's beef, pork and sausages are available throughout the county.

1671 Salem Road, Consecon | 613-965-6381 | www.waltssugarshack.ca

Alpacas at The SHED

HILLIER

Hillier House

Objets d'art and objects of desire in a quaint, historical little shop that once catered to Sir John A.

18646 Loyalist Parkway, Hillier | 613-399-2842 | www.hillierhouse.ca

Prince Edward County Lavender

In June, the first whiffs of that distinctive aroma start drifting across the fields. By July, when the plants are in full bloom, all of Closson Road is bathed in a lavender scent and cars can't help but pull in to the farm. The seasonal boutique stocks lavender-infused everything from bath oil to balms, sugar to vinegar. There are even three B&B rooms available for the most dedicated lavender enthusiasts; just be sure to book early if you want to visit during the annual lavender festival weekend in early July.

732 Closson Road, Hillier | 613-399-1855 | www.peclavender.com

The SHED at Chetwyn Farms

Elegant clothing and accessories created from fine alpaca fleece in a beautifully renovated chicken coop. See more about The SHED on page 141. (Seasonal only; call ahead to confirm hours.)

500 Closson Road, Hillier | 613-399-1990 | www.chetwynfarms.com

Prince Edward County Lavender

New Fiction

PRINCE EDWARD COUNTY

FICTION

Books & Company

PICTON

Books & Company

A little girl reads *Goodnight Moon* to her stuffed monkey in the kids' section while her mother browses the paperbacks. A book club is discussing their latest read over maple scones at Miss Lily's Café, and there's a cat named Pushkin curled up in a pool of sunlight in the front window. A great selection of new and used books, including an invaluable section dedicated to the county, yes, but this store is also a hub for the social, intellectual and literary life of the whole region. Books & Company is living proof that the local, independent bookstore still has an important role to play in the life of a community.

289 Main Street, Picton | 613-476-3037 | www.pictonbookstore.com

Gilbert and Lighthall Marketplace

Back in the nineteenth century, this was where locals looking for new cabinets or furniture—or even a quality coffin—shopped. Today it's a sprawling housewares store in a recently restored 120-year old landmark building.

171/173 Main Street, Picton | 613-476-3131 | www.gilbertandlighthall.com

Zest Kitchen Shop

Everything the well-stocked kitchen and bar require in a bright, welcoming space. Jen and Kyle stock only the best: pots, pans and knives, of course, but also bright lunchboxes for the kids, locally made dish towels and books (wink).

192 Main Street, Picton | 613-645-9378 | www.zestkitchenshop.com

PRINCE EDWARD

The Local Store

Handmade dolls to hot sauce. Pottery to cheese. Soap to nuts. If it's made in the county, cooked in the county or crafted in the county, there's a good chance you'll find it at this beautifully renovated old Loyalist barn on the road to Sandbanks. Arts and crafts are featured in the old milking parlour. The former lambing barn is where you'll find spices and snacks, while upstairs in the brightly lit hay loft, antiques and oil paintings get pride of place. Janice and Gary Scharf have curated what is easily the biggest collection of county handiworks in one place.

768 County Road 12, Prince Edward | 613-393-1797 | www.local-pec.com

Frugal & Company

The Local Store

Shauna Seabrook and Ted Pickering

Festival Players of
Prince Edward County

TASTEMAKER PROFILE

◇◇◇◇◇◇◇◇◇◇◇◇◇◇◇◇◇◇◇◇◇

Shauna Seabrook & Ted Pickering

"This chicken coop is nicer than my apartment," a visiting hipster from the city announces as she walks into The SHED. Owners Shauna Seabrook and Ted Pickering have transformed the old coop on their farm into a shop filled with all the things that speak to a life well lived: cozy throws, comfortable sweaters, warm slippers, alpaca poo.

Admittedly, alpaca poo might not be high on everyone's list of must-have home lifestyle items, but when you own and operate an alpaca farm, you learn a few things. Things like, alpaca manure makes an excellent soil enhancer.

The Seabrook and Pickering pair might seem an unlikely couple to own and operate an alpaca farm—she works in health care, he's a retail consultant. If it wasn't for the charms of one particular nineteenth-century farmhouse, they might never have become farmers in the first place. "Originally, we were looking for waterfront property," Seabrook says, "but when we saw this farm, something clicked."

It was important to the couple that the 55-acre parcel retain its farm designation, but in order to do that, they would have to actually farm the property. Seabrook fondly remembered visits to an alpaca farm when she was growing up and thought that might be the solution. "We wanted to start with just three," she says, "but came home with five." Today, 15 elegant alpacas roam the farm.

The alpacas might be what the couple is best known for, but it's a small part of the contribution they make. "One of the things that drew us here was the opportunity to be involved with the arts community," Seabrook says. To that end, Seabrook is the chair of the Festival Players of Prince Edward County theatre company. "It's the only professional theatre company in the county. This is our eleventh season and we just hired a new artistic director, Graham Abbey, a director and actor from Stratford, who has a new vision that we're really excited about."

Additionally, Seabrook served on the board of the County Community Foundation while Pickering, along with a few neighbours, created an organization to promote the various businesses along Closson Road, where they live. Both, of course, are active in the local alpaca community.

"This is an amazing place," Shauna says. "There are so many ways to join together to make a difference."

Blizzmax Gallery

GALLERIES
BLOOMFIELD

Cranston Gallery

Mixed media from a talented family. Sharon Fox Cranston's harmonious, pastel landscapes; her husband, Guy Cranston's found object sculptures; and paintings from the late Toller Cranston give this elegant little gallery a broad appeal.

185 Main Street, Bloomfield | 613-393-3900 | www.cranstongallery.com

Oeno Gallery

For fans of contemporary Canadian art, this modern gallery and its accompanying four-acre sculpture garden on the grounds of Huff Estates winery are as big a draw to the county as a trip to Sandbanks or a taste of local Pinot. For many artists, an exhibition here is a career highlight. Owner Carlyn Moulton's keen eye for modern paintings, sculpture, glassworks and digital art has helped make this gallery one of Ontario's finest.

2274 County Road 1, Bloomfield | 613-393-2216 | www.oenogallery.com

Oeno Gallery

PICTON

Arts on Main Gallery

This artist-run mixed media gallery features everything from weaving to photography, pastels to quilts.

223 Main Street, Picton | 613-476-5665 | www.artsonmaingallery.ca

Blizzmax Gallery

For a quarter century, Alice and Peter Mennacher's old barn overlooking South Bay has hosted some of the county's most eclectic and dynamic contemporary art shows. Installations might pair furniture with etchings, photography with poems, or sculpture with aquatints.

3071 County Road 13, Picton | 613-476-7748 | www.blizzmax.com

Mad Dog Gallery

Light floods in through the tall windows of this beautifully refurbished, timber-framed century barn. Spotlights further illuminate the space, picking out individual works that glow against the wood walls. Since 1990, the gallery, and its 25 acres of winding, sculpture-filled trails on the shore of East Lake, has showcased the best local artists. Rich, evocative landscapes from local artists like Rosemary Brown, Susan Straiton and Elizabeth Jackson-Hall are joined by ceramics from Bill Redick, fluid, dynamic sculptures by Tarmo Aun and the dreamlike canvasses of Andrew King.

525 County Road 11, Picton | 613-476-7744 | www.maddoggallery.ca

Maison Depoivre

Art gallery and food boutique, or food gallery and art boutique, Vincent Depoivre and Christophe Doussot's 150-year-old farmhouse provides a home for both. Featured artists change every couple of months, but there's always a selection of the finest gourmet ingredients available in the shop: chocolate, olive oil, and mustard from France.

Loch Sloy Business Park, Barrack 3, 343 County Road 22, Picton | 647-381-9407 | www.maison-depoivre.ca

Small Pond Arts

Krista Darby and Milé Murtanovski call their 87-acre property an "art farm." The small gallery next to the house is packed with Murtanovski's romantic paintings of everyday objects, places and people, but there's even more to see outside among the walking trails. On any given day, visitors might find a build-your-own scarecrow festival taking place, musicians performing and recording in the old silo or a puppet show happening behind a cardboard box in a field.

337 Clarke Road, Picton | 613-471-1322 |
www.smallpondarts.ca

The UnGallery

With a roster of more than 40 contributing artists in just about every imaginable medium—abstract landscapes to folk art flags, hand-carved bowls to handcrafted jewellery—this is a favourite one-stop art shop for the aesthetically inclined.

129 Main Street, Picton | 613-645-3033 |
www.theungallery.ca

Small Pond Arts

Mariners Park Museum

MUSEUMS
MILFORD

Mariners Park Museum

The stone lighthouse that dominates the grounds, a memorial to the many sailors from the county who lost their lives at sea, serves as a beacon, drawing visitors to this charming museum that details the county's deep nautical history. Shipbuilders, rum runners, fishermen and ice harvesters all made their mark and are honoured here. Give the foghorn a blast and scan the treasures salvaged from the hundreds of shipwrecks that lie buried beneath the waves around the county. Fort Kente, a recreated fort from the War of 1812 era, is also on the grounds and makes a great spot for a picnic.

2065 County Road 13, Milford | 613-476-2148 ext. 2525

Macaulay Heritage Park

PICTON

Macaulay Heritage Park

The smell of horses still lingers in the old stables and, for those who listen carefully, the echoes of the choir can still be heard in the original Church of St. Mary Magdalene. A fire burns in the hearth, as it has for centuries, tended by a fellow in red suspenders and a straw hat, while a plump woman in a bonnet and apron makes tea. Don't worry, they aren't ghosts, but volunteers with some good stories to share about this place and its original inhabitants. Named for Reverend William Macaulay, a missionary, philanthropist and all-around beloved figure in the county back in the early nineteenth century, this collection of heritage buildings, gardens and parkland transports visitors back to the early days of the Loyalist development of the county.

35 Church Street, Picton | 613-476-2148 ext. 2524

Rose House Museum

Little has changed in this old farmhouse since it was first occupied by Loyalist Peter Rose, one of Marysburgh's first settlers, back in the early 1800s. Today, the house stands as a living reminder of the county's rich history and gives visitors a feel for how life was lived 200 years ago.

3333 County Road 8, RR4, Picton | 613-476-5439

WELLINGTON

Wellington Heritage Museum

The museum's home, originally a Quaker meeting house, was built in 1885 just as the local canning industry, which this museum so lovingly pays tribute to, was getting started. Canada's first fruit- and vegetable-canning factory was built nearby in Picton toward the end of the nineteenth century. By the 1950s, the county boasted more than 75 such factories, which were a major part of the local economy. McCaws Peas, Lasso brand tomatoes, Lion Brand Sugar Corn and dozens of other brands were sent around the world. The Douglas A. Crawford canning collection honours the man considered the father of the Canadian canning industry.

290 Main Street, Wellington | 613-476-2148 ext. 2526

Macaulay Heritage Park

ALSO NOTABLE

99.3 County FM

There's an irresistible, scrappy energy to this eclectic, volunteer-run radio station. All the local news, from potato race highlights to rare bird sightings, and a music selection unconstrained by pre-programmed playlists. Expect to hear everything from Modern English to Miles Davis, sometimes in the same set! See more about County FM on page 231.

613-476-2229 | www.993countyfm.ca

The Bean Counter Café

Breakfast, lunch and comfort. Maybe the best place in the county for an affogatto (gelato with a shot of espresso poured over it). For those who can't make it in to one of the three locations, beans are available at local shops for home-brewing.

172 Main Street, Unit 101, Picton | 613-476-1718 | www.beancountercafe.com

City Revival

First choice for the county's fashionistas for more than 25 years. Recycled designer duds from around the world: t-shirts to trench coats, slingbacks to snow shoes.

275 Main Street, Picton | 613-476-7445 | www.cityrevival.com

Cooke's Fine Foods & Coffee

The original Kingston store has kept customers in exotic ingredients for more than 150 years. The Picton outpost dates to the 21st century but still offers the same great selection of kitchenwares, ingredients and tools that made the original famous.

280 Main Street, Picton | 613-476-2888 | www.cookesfinefoods.com

Heart of the County

Eclectic gift store affiliated with Community Living Prince Edward, a local nonprofit that offers employment and support to developmentally challenged young men and women.

183 Main Street, Picton | 613-476-1242

Kingston Olive Oil Co.

Can't tell an arbequina from a sevillano? Learn all about it and more at this county outpost of the popular olive oil, vinegar and gourmet foods store. There's even a tasting bar for sampling.

185 Main Street, Picton | 613-546-5483 | www.kingstonoliveoil.com

Mustang Drive-In

Who needs Dolby Ultra Imax 4D with surround sound when you've got fresh air, clear skies and warm popcorn under the stars? They've been showing movies at the Mustang for more than 60 years and in that time whole generations have built memories here. Much of its continued appeal can be chalked up to Paul and Nancy Peterson who bought the theater 30 years back. Today, kids in pyjamas clamber over the climbing equipment and scamper up and down the slide on the playground that's set up just in front of the screen, so parents can keep one eye on *Spider-Man* and another on the kids on the monkey bars. It's easy to imagine those boys and girls will grow up and watch over their own kids at this same spot one day.

1591 County Road 1, Picton | 613-393-2006 | www.thechequesinthemail.com

Taste Your World

Exotic ingredients from around the globe from Sarawak to Singapore and back. Always the first stop for hard-to-find international ingredients.

181 Main Street, Picton | 613-476-6465

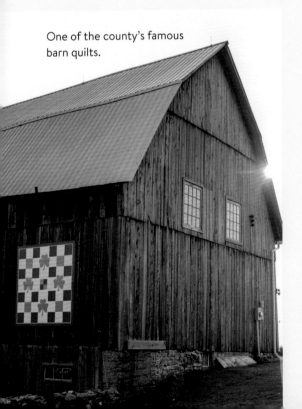

One of the county's famous barn quilts.

TASTEMAKER PROFILE

◇◇◇◇◇◇◇◇◇◇◇◇◇◇◇◇◇◇◇◇◇◇◇◇

Chrissy Poitras and Kyle Topping

Fantastic and slightly dangerous-looking old machines, with giant flywheels and felt rollers and razor-sharp blades, dominate the tidy workshop at Chrissy Poitras and Kyle Topping's Spark Box Studio headquarters. Walls are filled with framed work, much of it from the various artists-in-residence who have come from around the world to stay and work here. Old milk crates house dozens of books on the finer points of print making and etching and silk screening.

Poitras and Topping's work is deeply influenced by life in Prince Edward County; she's seventh generation, and that is reflected in their home and personal style. They've seen big changes happen in the county in the past ten years, not just in terms of more visitors and artists seeking out the area, but also in the overall aesthetic. "I feel like the aesthetic of the county used to be kind of redneck, but now there's this kind of rustic Canadiana," Poitras says. "I think there's a lot of people who have moved here who want to have the luxuries of a city with the benefits of a small town, and so that morphs into a kind of nostalgic and cute version of Canadiana."

"And it generally has barn board," Topping adds.

EGGS

Self Serve eggs
Chicken - Duck - Goose
Prices Marked
Free Range = Candled

Farm Stands & Farmers' Markets

BLOOMFIELD

Everdean Farms

The Rutgers have farmed this land for 30 years and, in addition to the usual complement of tomatoes, sweet corn, potatoes and beans, they grow beautiful flowers and bedding plants.

13791 Loyalist Parkway, Bloomfield |
613-476-2646

Kleinsteuber Farms

Look for the sign that says "Pickeling vegies" and "Miny Corn." They're not much for spelling, but they grow some bee-yootiful froots and veggies. This fourth-generation family farm sells four kinds of corn, as well as cantaloupe, rutabaga and rhubarb, and much more. It's also a great place for bedding plants and hanging baskets. A stop at the farm gate on the road to Sandbanks is a tradition for generations of visitors.

1102 County Road 12 West Lake, Bloomfield |
613-393-5671

Portico Gardens

Specializing in organic vegetables, there's always something unexpected waiting at Portico. Look for sorghum popcorn balls, rainbow-coloured Glass Gem corn, Japanese shishito peppers and a basket's worth of heirloom tomatoes, such as

German Orange Strawberry, Lucid Gem and Marianna's Peace.

1475 County Road 2, Bloomfield |
www.porticogardens.ca

Schroedter's Farm Market

To call the homemade doughnuts that are the specialty here the best in the county will probably upset a few people. There are those who will insist they're the best in Ontario, others the best in Canada, and for some, the greatest in the world. While the doughnuts are a big draw, there are also some fine cakes, pies and preserves, along with soup and sandwiches.

1492 Highway 62, Bloomfield | 613-393-2823 |
www.schroedtersmarket.com

Van Grootheest Farms

Beyond an assortment of especially good-looking fruits and vegetables (how do they get their cabbages so plump?) there are fresh almond tarts, buckets of gladioli and a pair of cute horses watching over the proceedings.

48 Stanley Street, Bloomfield | 613-393-2077

CARRYING PLACE

The Campbell's Orchards

The season starts with the blossom-viewing hay rides in the spring and that leads into the strawberry social in early summer, while in autumn, when the corn is high, it's time to get lost in the corn maze. And, all year-round, there's fresh-pressed apple cider, ice cream, baked goods, Ontario peanuts and some of the county's best candy apples.

1633 County Road 3, Carrying Place | 613-962-3751 | www.campbellsorchards.com

The Campbell's Orchards

MILFORD

The Local Food Shop

Amor and Joaquim Conde are unlikely farmers. An architect and an automotive mechanic respectively, the pair gave up city life to dedicate themselves to all things county. In addition to farming they operate this cool little food shop in a century-old barn on the edge of their property (Amor's Antiques occupies the other barn). The Condes are dedicated to celebrating all the best products of the county, and their store includes offerings from Pyramid Ferments, Angelo Bean's sausages, and pickles from Portland Bridge Pickling Society, as well as their own produce, including goji berries, and organic olive oil that Joaquim imports from Portugal.

212 County Road 16, Milford | 416-451-8395 | www.thelocalfoodshop.ca

Vicki's Veggies

Who wouldn't want to eat a Golden Egg, or pop a Black Cherry or get a Little Lucky? The names of the more than 200 varieties of heirloom tomatoes grown on this lush farm are as distinctive and clever as the fruits are beautiful and delicious. Five minutes outside of Milford and just edging up against the Black River, off a street shaded by trees, Vicki's Veggies occupies 20 of the richest, most bucolic acres anywhere.

81 Morrison Point Road, RR2, Milford | 613-476-7241 | www.vickisveggies.com

Blue Wheelbarrow Farm

PICTON

Blue Wheelbarrow Farm

Anyone who has eaten in a restaurant in Prince Edward County in the past couple of years has probably had some of farmer Aaron Armstrong's vegetables. A relative newcomer—he only started farming in 2016—he's already a favourite with the county's top chefs. In addition to the usual, if unusually delicious carrots, peas and tomatoes, Blue Wheelbarrow grows all the cool stuff: mizuna, kohlrabi, French filet beans, purslane and, of course, kale. The small farm stand works on an honour system.

170 County Road 32, Picton | 613-827-1614

Creasy's Apple Dabble Farm

With names like classic paintings—Flemish Beauty, Northern Spy, Tolman Sweet, Early Yellow, Mount Royal and Stanley Prune—there's a dozen types of apples to be found here, and seasonal vegetables are offered when they're ripe.

3091 County Road 8, RR4, Picton | 613-476-5142

Fosterholm Farms

Right on the edge of Sandbanks Provincial Park, they've been producing top-drawer fruit and vegetables, maple syrup and pussy willows on this 1,500-acre farm for close to a century. A small fridge under one of the tents holds Black River Cheese Company's Maple Cheddar that utilizes maple syrup from the farm.

2234 County Road 18, Picton | 613-393-5655

Greenridge Farms

It was front-page news when an ill-timed cold snap destroyed former owner Bryan Beatty's asparagus crop back in 2010. Things eventually warmed up and the season was saved, but it was a close call for the farm. These days, the prime plots are under the care of farmer Sandi Greer, who makes sure that every spring there's fresh stalks available for the generations of families for whom picking up some of the season's best asparagus straight from the farm is a long-time tradition.

1001 Ridge Road, Picton | 613-393-2986

Hagerman Farms

For more than 100 years, the baskets of produce beside the big red barn at Hagerman Farms have tracked the seasons as closely as an almanac. First to arrive are asparagus, plump and tender. Cucumber, onions, peas and cherries are next. By mid-summer, the red shelves are heavy with baskets: snow-white cauliflower, dirt-caked beets, tomatoes in every shape, size and colour, berries and melons galore. Autumn brings whole patches worth of pumpkins—some as big as a toddler—that spill out onto the surrounding yard. Squash with mysterious names—pepper, Jamaican and celebration—join kale, leeks and plums until the farm can barely contain it all. The smell of baked pies wafts out from the farm store. Jams, jellies and whole pecks-worth of homemade pickles make sure nothing goes to waste. Save a few minutes to visit the farm animals out behind the herb garden.

13644 Loyalist Parkway, Picton | 613-476-5362

Haystrom Farm

Former chef Jim Hayward brings a culinary sensibility to his 58-acre plot of exotic fruits and heirloom vegetables. With more than 400 varieties throughout the season, there's always something new to try.

578 Bethel Road, RR8, Picton | 613-471-1672

Honey Wagon Farms

Asparagus to zucchini and just about everything in between are all grown here without the use of herbicides, fungicides or pesticides. The farm's delectable maple syrup, collected in buckets, boiled over a wood-fired evaporator and filtered through felt, in the time-honoured way, is some of the finest in the county.

265 Sandy Hook Road, Picton | 613-476-6191

Mill Creek Farm

The farm that peas built. A small test plot back in the mid-80s has grown into one of Ontario's largest suppliers of fresh peas. You'll find lots of them here in season, along with all kinds of fresh produce, fresh baked pies and farm preserves.

44 County Road 11, Picton | 613-476-7709 | www.millcreekfarm.ca

WAUPOOS

The Blueberry Patch
Blueberries are the namesake but the big, open field is filled with berries of all kind: straw, rasp and black, throughout the season.

2984D County Road 8, Waupoos | 519-458-8066 | www.theblueberrypatch.ca

Little Highbush Blueberries
This third-generation family farm's been growing blueberries since 1978.

3214 County Road 8, Waupoos | 613-471-1353

WELLINGTON

Lakeshore Farms Market

"Good Things Grow Here," reads the sign, and that includes all manner of fruits and vegetables, local maple syrup and honey. In season, visitors can pick their own strawberries, and out of season the freezer is always filled with sausages and steaks, quiches and onion rings and farm-picked frozen vegetables.

467 Main Street, Wellington | 613-399-1733

Wellington Farmers' Market

As much of a Saturday tradition for some folks as sleeping in and doing the crossword. Novelty gourds, homemade bread, artisanal vinegar, the Wellington Farmers' Market brings all the bounty of the county together in one convenient location. During the week it's a parking lot for the United Church, but come Saturday, the tents are raised, the musicians start jamming and the market comes to life. Be sure to visit Sam at The Shore Oysters for a fresh-shucked Malpeque or two, grab a warm loaf of Wilson Road Rye from Henry straight out of the wood oven at the Humble Bread stand, and pick up whatever's in season from Lakeshore Farms.

243 Main Street, Wellington

Hagerman Farms

TASTEMAKER PROFILE

◇◇◇◇◇◇◇◇◇◇◇◇◇◇◇◇◇◇

Kate Golding

Artist and designer Kate Golding takes elements of the county—the cedar trees of Chuckery Hill Road, Picton's Crystal Palace, the sand dunes—and turns them into functional art. A sketch of a pack of coyotes might get printed on an organic hemp pillow. A colourful collection of heirloom tomatoes could become a set of napkins. Turkey vultures or a plump bunch of strawberries might show up as wallpaper. In fact, you can see many of her beautiful designs on these very pages.

Golding's a relatively recent transplant, having only moved to Canada from the UK in 2000, and to the county in 2012, but that newness helps her see the area with fresh eyes. We spoke just ahead of the launch of her latest collection, The Great Lakes, and I asked what it is about the county that inspires her.

"I love the landscape and the geography of the area," she explains. "Whether it's the beach, or the rocky coastline, or the agriculture, or the trails, or Macaulay Mountain, there are so many different facets to enjoy and be inspired by."

She also cites the community of artists and entrepreneurs, some of whom have lived here for generations, others who are only arriving now, as a source of inspiration. "I think there's a real collective enthusiasm for people who are making things," she says, "whether you're an artist or a chef or a musician."

Her new collection includes prints inspired by blue jays and another featuring loons in dappled water. Golding says that both designs are from specific personal experiences that had an impact. "In my life and in my work, it's important to feel the joy of those little things, those simple pleasures," she says, "and I wanted to share that personal joy of these elements that I see around me."

I asked Golding to describe what, for her, would constitute a perfect day in the county. "I'd start with a coffee from Miss Lily's, enjoyed in the parkette overlooking Picton Harbour," she says without hesitation. "Then I'd probably do some antiquing. Maybe go to MacCool's Re-Use to check out some bargains. And then a long walk either at Macaulay Mountain or the sand dunes, followed by pizza and a glass of wine at Norman Hardie. I would probably end the day by watching the sunset at Little Bluff."

Suggested Itineraries

Understanding that no traveller can be so easily encapsulated into one type, feel free to mix and match from the suggestions listed below.

THE ROMANTIC

Where to Stay

There are only seven rooms at **The Manse** in Picton, but they are all romantic in their own way. Besides, the outdoor pool, hot tub, wraparound veranda and in-house spa means that, if you are otherwise occupied, you never have to leave the grounds.

What to Do

At **Grange of Prince Edward Vineyards & Estate Winery**, wander down the shaded laneways, through the vines, or in among the woods. With more than 500 acres to choose from, it's not hard to find a quiet place to lay out your blanket. Starting on weekends in May, then every day through the summer, the winery offers delicious little picnic baskets with everything you need to make a day of it: basket, blanket and bread, of course, but also local cheese and charcuterie, homemade pickles and even a glass or two of wine.

As the old song says, "You'll look sweet upon the seat of a bicycle built for two." The good folks at **Bloomfield Bicycle Company** rent them—they're called tandem bikes now, BTW—and will even throw in a riding map to make sure you only travel on the most bucolic of back roads.

If ever there was a view to inspire amorous thoughts, it's found looking out past the verdant orchards across to Lake Ontario from the patio of the **County Cider Company**. There are wood-fired pizzas, cider cocktails, and umbrellas for shade.

The couple that cooks together stays together. The kitchen is one of the best places in the house to get creative and a cooking class at **From the Farm Cooking School** (www.fromthefarm.ca) always gets the juices flowing. From amateur to artiste, everyone can pick up some tips and, as a bonus, there's a great meal at the end.

Husband and wife artists Tara Wilkinson and Andrew Csafordi's **Love Nest Studio Gallery** (www.loveneststudios.com) is both grand and intimate. The restored chicken coop is where you'll find fibre art sculptures and photography, while the 100-year-old barn houses original encaustic paintings.

Insider Tip

Room number seven at The Manse, overlooking the pool and hot tub, is the quietest and doesn't share any walls with any other rooms. Do with that information what you wish.

THE URBANITE

Where to Stay

The style-conscious choice for accommodation in the county is always the **Drake Devonshire**. There's yoga in the mornings, art on the walls, and a mixologist behind the bar. All the comforts of home in a lakeside setting.

What to Do

Bloomfield isn't exactly known for its cutting-edge nightlife, but **The Hayloft Dancehall** (www.thehayloftdancehall. com) in nearby Cherry Valley is gaining a reputation well outside of the island as a legendary place to dance to live music. Catch a classic from your youth or discover a new favourite. Roots, blues, and good old rock and roll mean there ain't no party like a Hayloft party 'cos a Hayloft party has hay-bale seats.

Beer halls are the new taco trucks and the cool kids are lining up for saison and charcuterie at **County Road Beer Company**. Picnic tables on the patio overlook Hinterland Wine Company's Pinot Noir and Chardonnay vines, while seats inside have a view into the open kitchen.

Proving that culture isn't just for city folk, the program line-up at the historic, beautifully renovated, art-deco, **Regent Theatre** (celebrating its 100th anniversary in 2018 with events planned throughout the year) (www.theregenttheatre.org) runs the gamut. First-run art house movies, naturally, but also live music and satellite broadcasts of live performances of opera, theatre, and lectures from London's National Theatre, New York's Metropolitan Opera and all the great stages of the world.

For a quarter century, artists Alice and Peter Mennacher have curated and occasionally starred in, some of the finest art exhibits the county has ever seen. Sculpture, installations, oil and ink, the couple's big barn studio, called **Blizzmax Gallery** near Milford, has seen it all.

The Rolling Stones sing about love and hope and sex and dreams on the stereo system, while cooks peel some of the best pizza this side of Napoli out of the big brick oven on the wide, warm patio at **Norman Hardie's**. Pair a salsiccia pizza, topped with a local salami from Angelo Bean, with a glass of County Cabernet Franc, or a tarte flambée with the famous County Chardonnay.

Insider Tip

The Hayloft operates an end-of-night shuttle back to Wellington, Bloomfield and Picton. For those who don't have a designated driver, the smart play is to taxi out there and catch the shuttle back.

Norman Hardie's

County Road Beer Company

THE EPICURE

Where to Stay

Everything comes together: rooms, service and, of course, food at the historic **Merrill Inn**. Make dinner reservations at the restaurant for the first night you arrive to help unwind after the journey, and again on the last night, because chef Michael Sullivan's food is too good not to taste twice.

What to Do

Make a tour of the county's unofficial signature dishes: the Big Bay Breakfast at the **Lighthouse Restaurant**, chicken and waffles at the **Drake**, a po'boy sandwich at **PicnicPEC**, chickpea fries served with garlic aioli at **Blumen**, the Acoustic Jam Burger at **The Acoustic Grill** and campfire ice cream at **Slickers**.

The golden ticket for any serious connoisseur in the county is a seat in the barn for one of chef **Jamie Kennedy's Summer Dinner Series** events at his farm in Hillier (www.jamiekennedy.ca/pages /dinner-series). Most of the ingredients come from Kennedy's own gardens, and there's always a local winemaker on hand to provide pairings and give insights into the unique challenges and joys of making wine in a cool climate.

A full day with **Prince Edward County Wine Tours** (www.pecwinetours.com) hits at least half a dozen spots—more if you're

quick, fewer if you find a nice patio.

Back in the day, Wellington's Midtown meat plant was the biggest employer in the county. Its new incarnation as the **Midtown Brewing Co.** also keeps a fair few people employed, albeit in much happier circumstances.

Pick up a taste of the county's best produce at any of the dozens of roadside farm stands that line the county side roads. The farmers themselves are often too busy in the fields to stop by, so the honour system is the way to go. Bring home a dozen eggs, a fresh basket of berries, some melons, and the best heirloom tomatoes ever.

Insider Tip

Early September is just about the best time of year for produce in the county (no offence to asparagus, blueberry or pumpkin season), as most ingredients are at their peak. Not only are the farmers' markets bursting with produce at this time, the best local restaurants are spoiled for delicious things to cook with.

THE NATURE LOVER

Where to Stay

Even outdoorsy types like a little luxury now and then, so why not treat yourself to a bit of glamping at **Fronterra Farm, Camp & Brewery**? Luxury prospector tents, complete with a summer kitchen and ensuite bathroom, make tent life something special.

What to Do

Spot a spotted loggerhead shrike and listen for the croak of the chorus frog at the **Prince Edward Point National Wildlife Area**. In the spring and fall, hundreds of species of birds use the location as a resting ground during their annual migration. In the summer, it's one of the county's best places to swim, hike and generally soak up nature.

Practise your cross-draw stroke with a leisurely canoe down the **Black River**. Meandering for a pleasant six kilometres from the village of Milford out to Prince Edward Bay, the waterway flows past forest and farmland and marsh through some of the most scenic land in the county.

Hike, jog or snowshoe along the 46 kilometres of the **Millennium Trail**, built along an unused old Canadian Pacific rail line, as it winds across the county's most rural spots and straight through Consecon, Wellington, Bloomfield and Picton. Wildlife and gorgeous rural vistas punctuate the hike every step of the way.

Ponder the mysteries of **Lake on the Mountain**, a wonder of Ontario that sits 62 metres above Adolphus Reach. Is it, as the Mohawk First Nations believe, a Lake of the Gods, rife with spirits? A bottomless lake, as early settlers imagined? Or, as geologists would have us believe, a collapsed limestone sinkhole? Decide for yourself, then grab lunch at the nearby **Miller House Café & Brasserie**.

Don't let the big one get away. The lakes and bays of the county are teeming with walleye, northern pike, largemouth bass, and more.

Insider Tip

The Prince Edward Point Bird Observatory (www.peptbo.ca/sbf-2017.php) offers guided bird walks for a mere $5 most weekends during spring migration.

THE FAMILY

Where to Stay

The renovated motel rooms at **Angéline's Inn** are as cozy as they are stylish, and reasonable enough that the whole family can just about afford to have their own room. Larger, standalone spaces, like the cozy chalet and the coach-house loft, have separate bedrooms or pullout couches.

What to Do

No iPad or Xbox can possibly compete with the thrill of catching your first movie alfresco. But even the best movies at the **Mustang Drive-In** (www.mustangdrive-in.com) have a hard time competing with the swings and slide set up in front of the screen at this county tradition.

Plant an umbrella in the sand, set out your towels and settle in for a day at Sandbanks. The kids will happily splash in the water, wander across the dunes and race up and down the beach all day long. Just don't forget the sunscreen.

Let the kids loose at the **County Youth Park** (www.facebook.com/County-Youth-Park-111995048858523) where small ones can work the slides and swings, while older shredders catch some air at the skate park. Next door, the **Crystal Palace**, built in 1887, is quite possibly the last remaining example of this kind of structure first made famous by architect Joseph Paxton at London's Great Exhibition of 1851.

Grab a cone of roasted banana or pecan pie ice cream (it has real pie in it) at **Slickers Ice Cream** (www.slickersicecream.com) in Bloomfield or Picton.

Even the pickiest eaters will get a kick out of picking their own fresh fruit and vegetables. **Campbell's Orchards** is one of the best places in the county to give a kid a taste of life on a farm. There's usually something good to pick: strawberries and blueberries in the spring, raspberries and cherries in the summer, and apples in the fall.

Insider Tip

Mid-October is time for the annual Pumpkin Fest in Wellington. Start the day with a pancake breakfast in the town hall, catch the parade in the afternoon, then get ready for the great pumpkin weigh-off when winners from around Ontario and Quebec are up for awards. The biggest weigh in well over 680 kilograms.

THE COLLECTOR

Where to Stay

Home to the magnificent **Oeno Gallery**, and surrounded by the famous four-acre sculpture gallery, the **Inn at Huff Estates** is ground zero for contemporary art lovers in the county.

What to Do

Get lost amid the teak and vintage glass at **MacCool's Re-Use**. From the sublime (a black leather Barcelona daybed) to the ridiculous (a '70s black velvet crying baby painting), and everything in between. If you make it home without a complete set of antique cobbler's tools and a bucket of potato mashers, you're doing well.

Vases, bowls and ornaments are blown into shape right before your very eyes at the **Armstrong Glassworks** (http://armstrongglassworks.com/index.shtml). Glass artist Mark Armstrong works out of a 100-year-old feed mill and his creations are as bright and beautiful as they are delicate.

Set aside a couple of hours to stop by the best little bookstore in the county. There are always a few gems tucked away amid **Books & Company**'s shelves. Whether it's county history, philosophical treatises, or the latest bodice ripper, chances are if you want to read it, you'll find it here.

Pull over on the road to **Sandbanks** and wander amid the various outbuildings that make up **The Local Store**. Every imaginable kind of thing from quilts to sausages, all made by local artisans, is on offer.

Insider Tip

Art in The County (www.artinthecounty .com), an annual juried exhibition of the region's best artists that runs in late June through early July, is a three-week celebration of all things inspired. It's located in the gallery above Books & Company, and admission includes the right to vote on your favourite pieces.

THE HISTORIAN

Where to Stay

The Hayes Inn (www.hayesinnpec.com), originally built in 1838 as the Hayes Tavern, retains much of its original period charm, albeit with the full complement of modern conveniences. Moved from Consecon in 1973 and reassembled at its new perch in Waupoos overlooking Smith's Bay, the inn is a true part of county history.

What to Do

There are five terrific little museums in the county and while it might be too much to do them all in one day, you could if you started really early. But I think it's better to take it easy and appreciate all of them. If you hit up **Rose House** and **Macaulay Heritage Park** on the first day, then you can head up and over to **Mariners' Park Museum**, the **Wellington Heritage Museum** and the **Ameliasburgh Heritage Village** the next.

Once you've got your fill of museums and a good sense of the variety of history on offer, reward yourself with a selfie with Canada's first prime minister. A life-sized bronze statue of Sir John A. Macdonald out in front of the **Armoury** on Main Street in Picton celebrates the fact that as a young lawyer, the future PM won his first court case in the county.

Antique farm implements hang from the brick walls of the **Barley Room** pub in **The Waring House Inn**. Situated in a stone farmhouse that dates back to the 1820s, there's no more historic place to get a turkey club in all of the county.

Five of the county's six lighthouses can be visited (the sixth, Salmon Point, is privately owned). Check out **Scotch Bonnet Island, Point Petre, Prince Edward Point, False Duck Island** and **Main Duck Island** lighthouses. How many can you find?

Those Victorians really knew how to build a cemetery. **Glenwood Cemetery,** consecrated in 1873, covers a sprawling 62 acres and is crisscrossed by wide, avenue-lined streets. With its mature trees and lush gardens, the cemetery is as much a beautiful urban park as it as a final resting place for some of Prince Edward County's most renowned citizens. Don't miss the Stone Chapel, an Ontario Heritage Site, that dates back to 1901.

Insider Tip

Lakeshore Lodge Day at Sandbanks is held every August, but it might as well be August 1862. Sandbanks Park staff dress up in period clothes, there's lemonade and three-legged races, and the ever-competitive carry-a-potato-on-a-stick race.

TASTEMAKER PROFILE

◇◇◇◇◇◇◇◇◇◇◇◇◇◇◇◇◇◇◇

Jamie Kennedy

Women in gauzy sundresses and men in their summer best, glasses of sparkling wine in hand, stroll in small groups through a grassy field. The sound of children playing floats across from somewhere in the distance. At the end of the trail, at a small clearing overlooking the town of Hillier, chefs serve up french fries from a portable fryer, spread rich pâté over grilled bread and top crisp apple slices with cubes of luscious pork belly. This is what happens when one of Canada's best chefs invites you over for dinner.

It is hard to believe that chef Jamie Kennedy has only been operating his Summer Dinner Series, at his farm in Hillier, for two years. The event feels so in tune with the setting and the chef's aesthetic, and is so well received by guests, that it feels timeless. For Kennedy that sense of history is no accident. "It feels like something I've been doing forever," he acknowledges, "and in a way I have, I just haven't been doing it on the farm."

The farm in question, a 115-acre traditional farm, was once a sort of community hub for the area. Remnants of the old blacksmiths shop and mill are still visible and a host of outbuildings give the farm a kind of village within a village sense of place. Kennedy purchased the property more than 15 years ago at the recommendation of his friend, the writer and winemaker Geoff Heinrichs.

"One day I get a call from Geoff that the property next to his had come up for sale," Kennedy recalls. "I was planning to go to Montreal, so I brought my whole family along and we stopped in the county to tour the property. It was during lilac season and the lilacs were all in bloom and I just thought, 'my god this is ridiculous.'" The price by Jamie's own reckoning was really reasonable, but with a young family and a busy restaurant to run he didn't think buying a farm was in the cards. "To tell you the truth," he says, "we kind of did it as a lark. When they came back and accepted it, we were like, okay, now what?"

Sitting in the barn all these years later, surrounded by friends and family, watching as Kennedy and his crew put out the last plates of food, the answer to that question seems obvious. Kennedy's approach to food and cooking, honed over 30 years in the industry, has always been about celebrating the connection

to the land, about food procurement and developing local food culture through the use of ingredients. Bringing those ideas and concepts to fruition with a dinner series on the farm just underscores that commitment. "It seriously kind of creates something that's bigger, greater than the sum of its parts," he says. "It's very satisfying to me, it's very soul filling and it kind of allows me to practise the things I'm always talking about while acting as a gentle form of education as well."

Recipes

SALADE NIÇOISE

LILI SULLIVAN, POMODORO, WELLINGTON

This classic French recipe is a great way to showcase the terroir of the county. The pickerel is caught in the Bay of Quinte by Dewey Fisheries. The vegetables are from Laundry Farms and Hagerman Farms, where I get most of my produce for home and work. Hagerman's also supply the eggs for the salad. The Carriage House Cooperage makes fantastic barrel-aged vinegars, so all the ingredients are locally sourced with the exception of the capers, olives, anchovies and olive oil. To pair with the dish—especially if you're eating alfresco—try a fun wine like the Harwood Estate Vineyards North Beach Rosé, a bright berry-tasting blend of Frontenac Gris and Riesling.

Serves 4

SALAD

12 small new potatoes

1 lb (500 g) green or yellow beans

6 cups lightly packed mixed greens

Salt and freshly ground black pepper

4 boneless, skinless pickerel fillets

3 Tbsp canola oil

2 Tbsp unsalted butter

24 black niçoise or kalamata olives

12 cherry tomatoes, cut in half

4 large eggs, hard-boiled, peeled and quartered

½ cup drained capers

1 shallot, thinly sliced

4 anchovy fillets

½ cup finely chopped mixed fresh herbs
  (parsley, chives and/or dill)

VINAIGRETTE

⅓ cup red wine vinegar

1 Tbsp Dijon mustard

1 clove garlic, finely minced

1 tsp kosher salt

1 cup olive oil

Freshly ground black pepper

Cook the potatoes in a large pot of boiling, salted water until tender, 8 to 10 minutes. Remove the potatoes from the water with a slotted spoon and set on a plate to cool.

In the same pot, blanch the beans until tender but still crisp, 2 to 3 minutes. Drain the beans and run them under cold water to stop the cooking.

Meanwhile, make the vinaigrette. Combine the vinegar, mustard, garlic and salt in a bowl. Slowly whisk in the olive oil until the mixture has emulsified. Season with freshly ground black pepper to taste.

Once the potatoes have cooled, cut them in half and toss them in a bowl with about one-quarter of the dressing. Toss the greens in a second bowl with another one-quarter of the dressing, and season with salt and pepper to taste.

Next, prepare the pickerel fillets. Heat a large nonstick skillet over medium-high heat. Season the fish with salt and pepper on both sides. Add the canola oil to the hot skillet and put in the pickerel fillets, skin side down. Sear the fish by pressing down gently with a spatula. When the skin starts to lift from the skillet, the fish is ready to turn over. Flip the fillets, then add the butter to the skillet. Cook the fish for another 5 to 7 minutes, until cooked through. With a spatula, remove the fish to a cutting board.

While the fish is cooking, plate the salad. Divide the dressed mixed greens among four shallow bowls or plates. Arrange the dressed potatoes, the beans, olives, tomatoes and eggs on top of the greens. Sprinkle each salad with the capers and sliced shallot, and top with the anchovies.

Drizzle more dressing over the salads and place a piece of pickerel on top of each. Sprinkle with fresh herbs.

GOAT CHEESE & SPINACH-STUFFED EGGPLANT CANNELLONI WITH ZUCCHINI PATTIES & RED PEPPER SAUCE

CHEF ANDREAS FELLER, BLUMEN GARDEN BISTRO, PICTON

Ninety percent of the ingredients for this vegetarian dish can be purchased at a single farm stand during the summer season: one-stop shopping at its best. My favourite places are Hagerman Farms, Maple Brae Farm and Blue Wheelbarrow Farm. If the weather's bad, I also like the produce at County Sunshine Health Store in Picton. This would pair well with any number of drinks. The Farmhouse Saison from County Road Brewery or a crisp, unoaked Chardonnay like the ones from Sugarbush and Rosehall Run would work well. A Pinot Gris from Grange of Prince Edward or Casa-Dea would be an excellent choice, too.

Serves 4

EGGPLANT CANNELLONI

2 medium eggplant (about 8 x 4 inches/20 x 10 cm)

Salt

¼ cup olive oil, divided

Freshly ground black pepper

8 oz (250 g) spinach, thick stems trimmed

2 tsp finely chopped garlic

4 oz (125 g) fresh goat cheese

1 cup tomato juice

½ cup freshly grated Parmigiano-Reggiano

ROASTED MUSHROOMS

2 large or 4 small portobello mushrooms, stems removed and gills scraped out with a spoon

2 to 3 Tbsp balsamic vinegar

2 to 3 Tbsp olive oil

8 sprigs fresh thyme

Salt and freshly ground black pepper

ZUCCHINI PATTIES

4 cups grated green or yellow zucchini

Salt

1 medium onion, thinly sliced

2 Tbsp olive oil

2 tsp finely chopped garlic

⅓ cup all-purpose flour

1 large egg

3 tsp finely chopped mixed fresh herbs (thyme, rosemary, oregano and/or parsley)

Freshly ground black pepper

ROASTED PEPPER SAUCE

1 Tbsp olive oil

2 stalks celery, diced small

1 medium onion, diced small

1 medium carrot, diced small

2 tsp finely chopped garlic

4 sweet peppers (any colour but green),
     roasted, peeled, seeded and sliced

1 can (10 oz/284 mL) tomato juice

2 to 3 Tbsp freshly grated Parmigiano-Reggiano

2 Tbsp thinly sliced fresh basil leaves

GARNISH

Balsamic vinegar glaze

¼ cup pine nuts, toasted

¼ cup capers, fried until crisp then drained on
     paper towel

Freshly grated Parmigiano-Reggiano

First, prepare the eggplant. Preheat the oven to 350°F. Slice each eggplant lengthwise into ¼-inch (6 mm) slices, lay them in a single layer on a wire rack and salt them lightly.

After a few minutes, pat each eggplant slice dry, drizzle generously with some of the olive oil and sprinkle with salt and pepper to taste. Arrange in a single layer on a rimmed baking sheet, then roast in the oven until soft, 15 to 20 minutes. Remove from the oven and let cool, but leave the oven on.

Heat a large skillet over high heat. Add the remaining olive oil to the skillet, then add the garlic. It will start browning fairly quickly, so be careful. Once it starts browning a bit, add the spinach and move it around to pick up the garlic from the bottom. Before the spinach is completely wilted, season with salt and pepper to taste.

Once the spinach has wilted, remove the skillet from the heat and let the spinach cool to room temperature. Transfer the cooled spinach to a colander to drain, pressing to squeeze out excess liquid.

Crumble the goat cheese, trying to keep some of the chunks large. Add the goat cheese to the spinach and toss to combine.

To assemble the eggplant cannelloni, lay the roasted eggplant slices flat on a work surface. Spoon ⅓ cup of the spinach mixture on one end of each slice, then roll up the slices. Arrange the eggplant roll-ups in a baking dish. Spoon a couple of tablespoons of tomato juice over each one and sprinkle with Parmigiano-Reggiano.

For the roasted mushrooms, drizzle each one with balsamic vinegar and olive oil. Place them on a rimmed baking sheet. Top the mushrooms with the thyme sprigs and season with salt and pepper to taste. Roast until the centres are soft to the touch and juices begin to come from the mushrooms, about 8 minutes. Remove the mushrooms from the oven, but leave the oven on. Let the mushrooms cool to room temperature, then cut them into ½-inch (1 cm) slices. Set aside.

For the zucchini patties, put the grated zucchini in a bowl, sprinkle with salt and let stand for 15 minutes. Meanwhile, heat a large saucepan over medium heat. Add the sliced onion and olive oil. Cook, stirring frequently, for 5 minutes. Add the garlic and cook, stirring, for another 3 to 4 minutes. Try not to let the onions brown. Remove the saucepan from the heat.

Once the zucchini has drained for 15 minutes, squeeze it to eliminate as much liquid as possible. Place zucchini in a bowl. Add the cooked onion, flour, egg, herbs, and salt and pepper to taste and mix well.

Heat a nonstick skillet over medium heat. Spoon portions of zucchini mixture into skillet and pat out to form four 4-inch (10 cm) patties, about ½ inch (1 cm) thick. Cook for 2 minutes, then carefully flip them with a spatula and cook for 1 more minute. Transfer the patties to a baking sheet lined with parchment paper and bake them in the oven until they are firm to the touch, about 20 minutes.

For the roasted pepper sauce, heat the oil in a small saucepan over medium heat, and sweat the diced celery, onion and carrot for 5 minutes. Add the garlic, then cook, stirring, for 2 minutes. Add the roasted peppers, and cook, stirring often, for a couple more minutes. Add the tomato juice and bring to a simmer. Reduce the heat to low and simmer, uncovered, until slightly

thickened, about 30 minutes. If the mixture dries out too much, add a couple of tablespoonfuls of water or vegetable stock.

Remove the saucepan from the heat. Stir in the grated Parmigiano-Reggiano. The sauce should be fairly thick and the cheese will thicken it a little more and season it, so season sparingly with salt and pepper to taste. Stir in the basil.

To assemble the dish, preheat the oven to 350°F. Arrange the zucchini patties and eggplant rolls on a large rimmed baking sheet and reheat in the oven, about 10 minutes. Add the portobello mushrooms to the baking sheet and reheat, about 5 minutes. If needed, bring the roasted pepper sauce back to a simmer. Again, you can add water or vegetable stock if it is too thick.

To plate the dish, drizzle a fine circle of the balsamic glaze on four plates. Place a zucchini patty in the centre of each plate, and arrange two eggplant rolls on top of each patty. Place the sliced portobellos around each plate, and drizzle with the pepper sauce. Sprinkle each portion with toasted pine nuts and crisp capers. Top with grated Parmigiano-Reggiano to finish.

HOT SMOKED WHITEFISH WITH FENNEL & ONION SALAD

CHEF JAMIE KENNEDY, J. K. FARM, HILLIER

In Prince Edward County, we have a strong appetite for fish and fishing. Here we have the great Lake Ontario, the smaller lakes and streams. We are far from salt water and the dramatic tides of the sea. No matter; the lakes give us plenty. Whitefish is to the First Nations here as salmon is to the Aboriginals of the west coast. My recipe is inspired by the beautiful whitefish that swim in Lake Ontario and are indigenous to this region. I am fortunate to know Kendall Dewey, a local fisher who has observed and been involved in the conservation of the fishing industry for many years. He supplies me with excellent-quality whitefish. It is important for cooks living in locales similar to mine to look to the lakes for some or all of their supply of fish, wild or farmed. For this recipe, I smoke the whitefish. It lends itself well to this technique and the results are stunning, but if you don't have a smoker, you can always grill the fish.

Serves 6

SMOKED WHITEFISH

1 fresh whitefish (3 lb/1.5 kg), cleaned and
  filleted into two portions
1 Tbsp kosher salt
1 Tbsp granulated sugar
Green apple wood chips (not dry)

FENNEL AND ONION SALAD

1 medium red onion, thinly sliced
1 medium Spanish onion, thinly sliced
2 green onions, thinly sliced on the bias
1 head fresh fennel, cored and thinly sliced
¼ cup white wine vinegar
Salt and freshly ground black pepper
Good-quality bread and butter to serve

Season the flesh side of both fillets with salt and sugar, seasoning the fish as you would if you were going to pan-fry it. Place the fillets, flesh side up, on a plate and refrigerate for 4 hours, to let the fillets absorb the salt and sugar before smoking them.

After 4 hours, bring the temperature of the smoker to 200°F. Following the manufacturer's instructions, place the fillets and the green apple wood chips in the smoker. Smoke the fish for about 45 minutes. Remove the fish from the smoker and let cool for at least 2 hours in the fridge before eating.

Meanwhile, prepare the salad. Mix together the red, Spanish and green onions and fennel in a bowl. Add the vinegar, and salt and pepper to taste.

Place an equal amount of the salad on each of six plates. Slice the fish into six even-sized pieces and place, flesh side down, on top of each portion of salad. Peel off and remove the skin of each piece of fish. Serve with buttered bread.

HERB-POACHED CHICKEN WITH CREAMY MUSHROOM FRICASSÉE

CYNTHIA PETERS, FROM THE FARM COOKING SCHOOL, AMELIASBURGH

This recipe is a twist on a classic French dish. Almanac white wine, a refreshing blend of Chardonnay, Pinot Gris, and Riesling produced by Grange of Prince Edward, pairs well with Prinzen Farms chicken and balances nicely with the creamy fricassée packed with mushrooms from Highline Mushrooms, and kissed with Nyman Farms maple syrup.

For ease of prep, assemble and chop all the ingredients for both chicken and fricassée before you start cooking, then make the fricassée while the chicken is poaching.

Serves 4

HERB-POACHED CHICKEN

2 cups dry white wine

1 small onion, chopped

½ stalk celery, chopped

2 sprigs fresh rosemary, cut in half

A handful flat-leaf parsley

1 clove garlic

1 tsp black peppercorns

½ tsp kosher salt

4 boneless, skinless chicken breasts

CREAMY MUSHROOM FRICASSÉE

1 lb (500 g) shiitake mushrooms

4 Tbsp sunflower oil, divided

4 Tbsp unsalted butter, divided

½ cup finely chopped shallots

1 large tomato, cored and diced (juice reserved)

2 cloves garlic, finely chopped

1 cup reserved poaching liquid (from chicken)

⅓ cup dry white wine

2 Tbsp brandy

½ cup whipping cream

3 Tbsp maple syrup

1 tsp salt

½ tsp freshly ground black pepper

½ cup finely chopped flat-leaf parsley

Finely grated zest from ½ lemon

To poach the chicken, place 4 cups of cold water in a large, wide pot and add the white wine, onion, celery, rosemary, parsley, garlic, peppercorns and salt. Bring to a boil over high heat. Reduce the heat so the liquid is simmering, then gently slide the chicken breasts into the pot. Cook, watching carefully to ensure the liquid remains at a low simmer, until an instant thermometer inserted into the thickest breast registers 150°F, 12 to 15 minutes (cooking time depends on the size of the breasts).

When the chicken is done, use a slotted spoon to remove the breasts from the pot to a heatproof bowl. Pour enough liquid from the pot to cover the chicken (reserve remaining poaching liquid) and let the chicken breasts rest, uncovered, on the counter until the instant thermometer inserted into the thickest breast registers 160°F.

Meanwhile, make the fricassée. Gently wipe the mushrooms to remove any dirt, then remove and discard the stems. Slice the mushroom caps and place in a bowl.

In a large nonstick skillet, heat 1 tablespoonful each of oil and butter over medium-high heat. Place one-third of the mushrooms in the pan and let cook, without stirring, for 2 minutes. Stir the mushrooms and cook 1 minute longer. Remove the mushrooms from the pan and place in a bowl. Repeat the process, cooking the mushrooms in more two batches, adding more oil and butter to the skillet before cooking each batch and adding the cooked mushrooms to the bowl as each batch cooks.

Heat the remaining tablespoonful of oil and butter in the same skillet and sauté the shallots over medium heat until lightly golden, 3 to 5 minutes. Add the tomato and garlic, then cook for another few minutes. Add the reserved poaching liquid, wine and brandy. Bring to a simmer, then let simmer until the liquid has reduced by half.

Return the mushrooms to the skillet, along with the whipping cream, maple syrup, salt and pepper. Simmer, stirring occasionally, until the sauce has thicken slightly, about 6 minutes. Add half of the parsley and lemon zest. Simmer for 1 more minute. Taste and adjust the seasonings.

To serve, remove the chicken breasts from the poaching liquid and cut each on the diagonal into five or six slices. Use a slotted spoon to pile the mushroom mixture in the centre of each of 4 warm dinner plates. Arrange one sliced chicken breast on each plate. Spoon the cream sauce on top of each chicken breast and around each plate. Sprinkle the remaining parsley and lemon zest over each plate, then serve immediately.

CRISPY PICKEREL CHEEKS & WILD LEEK TARTAR SAUCE

NEIL DOWSON, COUNTY ROAD BEER GARDEN, HILLIER

Pickerel is one of my favourite fish to come out of the waters around the county, and the cheeks are an especially delicious treat. Wild leeks grow all around Hinterland's vineyards and I love to use them fresh when in season, but they pickle up nicely as well and make a great addition to a creamy tartar sauce. Pairing wise, I went with our Farmhouse Saison; it's made with cascade hops, which give it a nice fruit-citrus background plus, because it's bottle-conditioned, it has a nice amount of fizz that goes perfectly with the fish.

Serves 4 to 6

PICKLED WILD LEEKS

1 lb (500 g) wild leeks, thoroughly cleaned

1 cup cider vinegar

½ cup water

1 Tbsp salt

½ cup granulated sugar

1 bay leaf

WILD LEEK TARTAR SAUCE

3 large egg yolks

2 tsp lemon juice

2 tsp pickling liquid from wild leeks

1 tsp salt

1 tsp Dijon mustard

1 ½ cups olive oil

4 to 5 pickled wild leeks, coarsely chopped

3 shallots, finely chopped

2 Tbsp finely chopped flat-leaf parsley

1 Tbsp finely chopped tarragon

CRISPY PICKEREL CHEEKS

3 cups all-purpose flour, divided

1 cup cornstarch

1 bottle (650 mL) County Road Beer
     Farmhouse Saison, chilled

1 Tbsp table salt

Vegetable oil for deep-frying

24 pickerel cheeks

1 lemon, cut into 4 or 6 wedges

For the pickled leeks, put leeks in a large nonreactive bowl. Bring the vinegar, water and salt to a boil in a large nonreactive pot. Add the sugar and stir until dissolved. Add the bay leaf and pour over the leeks. Let cool completely, then transfer leeks and liquid into a large jar. Seal tightly and keep refrigerated for up to 1 month.

For the tartar sauce, place the egg yolks, lemon juice, pickling liquid, salt and Dijon

mustard in a food processor and blend for 2 to 3 minutes until the mixture has thickened. With the motor running, slowly add the oil until the mayonnaise is thick and glossy.

Add the pickled leeks, shallots, parsley and tarragon. Pulse once to combine, then transfer the tartar sauce to a bowl. Place in the fridge until needed.

To make the crispy pickerel cheeks, sieve 2 cups of the flour with the cornstarch into a large bowl. Add the beer and whisk until a thick batter forms. Place in the fridge until needed.

Sieve the remaining 1 cup of flour with the salt onto a large flat tray or platter.

Following the manufacturer's instructions, heat the oil in a deep-fryer to 375°F. Dredge the pickerel cheeks in the flour-salt mixture, then dip them in the cold beer batter to coat completely. Carefully slide the cheeks into the hot oil and cook until golden brown, 2 to 3 minutes.

Remove the cheeks from the fryer, drain well, then season with salt to taste. Serve with the wild leek tartar sauce and lemon wedges.

SMOKED ELK WITH WILDFLOWER HONEY GASTRIQUE & WILD RICE WITH MUSHROOMS & FIDDLEHEADS

MEGHAN VAN HORNE, THE PUBLIC HOUSE AT JACKSON'S FALLS, MILFORD

We get our elk from Century Game Park in nearby Warkworth, Ontario. Our honey comes from Honey Pie Hives and Herbals, just five minutes down the road where Bay Woodyard and Gavin North produce great honey and also make mead, teas and beauty products. Their monthly beekeeping workshops are also amazing. Highline Mushrooms in Wellington has been around for years and not only are their mushrooms good, but they also sell great soil in the spring.

The Pinotage from Del-Gatto Estates is an ideal pairing for this dish. Del-Gatto's is the first commercial planting of Pinotage in the county—and, I believe, in Ontario—grown from South African clones, so this is a pretty special wine! It has dark chocolate and espresso notes on the nose with brambly blue and dark red fruits on the palate. Finishing long, with sweet, elegant tannins and a touch of mocha, this wine stands up to the smoky flavour of the elk, without getting lost.

Serves 4 to 6

SMOKED ELK

1 Tbsp salt

1 tsp ground juniper or 4 tsp gin

1 elk tomahawk steak (2 to 3 lb/1 to 1.5 kg)

Apple wood chunks for smoking

WILD RICE

1 cup wild rice

1 lb (500 g) fiddleheads

3 Tbsp unsalted butter, divided

Salt

1 lb (500 g) seasonal mushrooms (we use morel and oyster)

GASTRIQUE

½ cup wildflower honey

½ cup cider vinegar

To prepare the elk, mix together the salt and ground juniper or gin. Coat the elk steak in the salt mixture, then seal it in a plastic bag, and let sit in fridge for 24 hours.

The next day, prepare your smoker. Bring the coals up to 200°F to 250°F (this should take about 1 to 1 ½ hours), then add a few chunks of apple wood. Add the elk steak to the smoker and smoke for 1 hour, turning it halfway through cooking time.

Meanwhile, make the wild rice by combining it with 4 cups of cold water in a large saucepan. Bring to a boil, then cover and reduce the heat to a simmer. Cook until the rice is tender, 35 to 45 minutes. Remove the rice from the heat and let it sit with the lid on for 15 minutes.

In a large saucepan, boil the fiddleheads in ½ cup of water until most of the liquid has evaporated, about 5 minutes. Add 1 tablespoonful of the butter and season with salt to taste. Sauté the fiddleheads until tender, about 15 minutes. Remove the fiddleheads from the saucepan and set aside.

In the same saucepan, sauté the mushrooms in the remaining butter until golden brown, about 10 minutes. Add the cooked wild rice and fiddleheads, and mix everything together in the saucepan.

For the gastrique, combine the honey and cider vinegar in a small saucepan and bring to a simmer for 10 minutes. Remove from the heat and let cool.

If needed, warm the smoked elk steak in a 400°F oven for 10 minutes. Slice the elk steak

in thick pieces, across the grain. Divide the wild rice among four or six dinner plates, and lay the slices of elk over it, then drizzle the gastrique over the top.

SECRET SANDWICH

REBECCA HUNT, PICNICPEC, WELLINGTON

This is basically our staff sandwich, and it's what we give our customers who love the sound of our fried chicken sandwich but don't eat meat. But we'll serve it to anyone if you give us the secret wink. In the county, we are blessed with a plethora of great produce farmers. This allows us to change our ingredients as they come and go in spring, summer and fall. Feel free to use whatever is available in your garden or local farmers' market.

We make our own pickled turnips with cumin seeds for a Mediterranean influence, and throw in a deep red beet for colour. We source our microgreens from Cloven Farm and our heirloom tomatoes from Vicki's Veggies or Blue Wheelbarrow Farm, a mere 10 kilometres away. For hot sauce, we use the one from Prince Edward County Hot Sauce Company in Original flavour. We love this sandwich with a nice glass of county white wine, or soda water mixed with County Yum Club Stinging Nettle-Rosemary Cordial—a super refreshing beverage, and a perfect complement to this sandwich.

Serves 4

QUICK PICKLED TURNIPS

½ cup kosher salt

2 bay leaves

2 lb (1 kg) turnips, peeled and cut into spears

1 cup distilled white vinegar

1 small beet, roughly chopped

2 cloves garlic, roughly chopped

1 tsp coriander seeds

1 tsp cumin seeds

SANDWICH

½ cup mayonnaise

2 Tbsp finely chopped chives (optional)

2 Tbsp lemon juice

1 clove garlic, finely grated

½ tsp celery seeds

½ tsp freshly ground black pepper

1 tsp vegetable or avocado oil

4 good-quality burger buns or large milk buns

8 slices halloumi cheese (¼ inch/6 mm thick)

1 large heirloom tomato, sliced

A handful of radish microgreens

20 spears pickled turnips

Hot sauce (optional)

For best flavour, make the quick pickled turnips about 5 days in advance. In a large nonreactive saucepan, heat 3 cups of water, and add the salt and bay leaves. Stir until the salt is completely dissolved, then turn off the heat. Add the turnips, vinegar, beet, garlic, and coriander and cumin seeds. Transfer the mixture to a large, nonreactive airtight container and store in the fridge for up to 1 month.

For the sandwich, make the seasoned mayo by combining the mayonnaise, chives, lemon juice and garlic in a bowl. Using a mortar and pestle or spice grinder, grind the celery seeds to a fine powder. Add the celery seeds and black pepper to the mayo, stir well and set aside.

Heat a skillet or plancha over medium-high heat. Add a tiny bit of oil (I use a paper towel to apply it directly on the pan). Throw your burger buns into the pan, cut sides down, until lightly toasted, 30 to 40 seconds. Remove the buns from the pan and set aside.

Place the halloumi slices in the pan, grilling them on each side for about 1 ½ minutes. While the halloumi is cooking, spoon a generous amount of the seasoned mayo on the top and bottom halves of the buns. Pile up the tomato slices and microgreens on the top halves. When the halloumi is ready, place it and the pickled turnips on the bottom halves, dividing evenly. Drizzle a bit of hot sauce on the halloumi if you like a little kick. Close the sandwiches and tuck in!

TARTIFLETTE

CHEF MATTHEW DEMILLE, EAT WITH MATT DEMILLE INTERACTIVE DINING & CULINARY CONSULTATION

Comfort food at its finest. During the cold winter months, who wouldn't want to dig into a bubbling dish of smoky bacon, sweet onions and melted cheese? Feel free to switch up the cheese depending on what you have available. Traditionally this is made with Reblochon but I like it with local cheese from Fifth Town. I've chosen Lighthall's Progression sparkling wine to go with the dish, as it's dry and crisp and cuts through the rich ingredients.

Serves 4

Kosher salt

4 to 6 medium Yukon Gold potatoes (1 ½ lb/ 750 g), scrubbed and thickly sliced

6 slices smoky bacon, cut into ¼ inch batons

1 medium onion, finely chopped

2 Tbsp finely chopped fresh thyme leaves

1 clove garlic, finely chopped

8 oz (250 g) Fifth Town Cape Cressy or Reblochon cheese, thinly sliced

Freshly ground black pepper

½ cup whipping cream

Pinch of grated nutmeg

Green salad and grilled sourdough bread to serve

Preheat the oven to 400°F. Place a large pot of water over high heat and bring to a boil. Season well with kosher salt. Add the potatoes and boil until the potatoes are soft but not falling apart, about 15 minutes.

Heat an 8-inch (20 cm) cast iron or ovenproof skillet over medium heat. Add the bacon and slowly fry it until it has rendered its fat and is golden brown.

Add the onion, thyme and garlic to the skillet, and continue cooking until the onion is soft. Remove the skillet from the heat and, with a slotted spoon, transfer the bacon mixture to a separate dish. Discard all but 1 tablespoonful of the fat in the skillet.

Layer the potatoes, bacon mixture and cheese in the skillet, seasoning each layer lightly with salt and pepper as you go. To finish, pour the cream over the potatoes, then sprinkle with the nutmeg. Bake in the oven until hot and bubbling, 10 to 15 minutes. Serve with a simple green salad and grilled sourdough bread.

SWEET CORN FLAN WITH ONTARIO SHRIMP, COUNTY SUCCOTASH & BACON VINAIGRETTE

CHEF SCOTT ROYCE, SEASONED EVENTS

This dish brings to mind that time when summer is turning to fall. The sweetness of the corn—I buy mine from Laundry Farms—is delicately offset by the smokiness of the paprika-seasoned shrimp, which come from First Ontario Shrimp, a shrimp farm in Campbellford, Ontario. The bacon vinaigrette rounds the palate and provides a sharp finish. The county succotash can easily be adjusted to use whatever ingredients are on hand throughout the seasons. I love the texture of this corn flan, but it also is a great base recipe that can be made with other vegetables. This dish is prep heavy, though much can be done the night before, and it will wow your guests. I think the flan goes beautifully with a glass of Norman Hardie's 2014 County Chardonnay. The wine's buttery, bright lemon notes pair beautifully with the complex flavours in this dish.

Serves 10

SWEET CORN FLAN

18 ears of corn

1 cup whipping cream

7 large eggs

2 large egg yolks

Small handful chives, thinly sliced

Salt and freshly ground black pepper

Olive oil, as needed

SHRIMP

30 peeled and deveined First Ontario shrimp

¼ cup smoked paprika (from Vicki's Veggies)

⅓ cup olive oil

Salt and freshly ground black pepper

SUCCOTASH

1 package (400 g) Mill Creek Farm Peas

3 Tbsp unsalted butter

1 small sweet red pepper, seeded and finely diced

1 shallot, finely chopped

½ cup white wine

2 bunches green onions, thinly sliced

BACON VINAIGRETTE

8 oz (250 g) bacon, finely diced

3 shallots, finely chopped

2 cloves garlic, minced

½ cup sherry vinegar

Salt and freshly ground black pepper

For the sweet corn flan, preheat the oven to 325°F and boil a kettle of water.

Remove the kernels from 12 of the ears of corn, reserving the remaining six ears. Process the corn kernels in a food processor, adding a little water if necessary, until a purée forms. Rub the purée through a sieve, discarding the solids in the sieve. You should have about 3 cups of corn cream.

In a large bowl, whisk together the corn cream and whipping cream. Whisk in the eggs and egg yolks. Stir in the chives.

Remove the kernels from three of the reserved ears of corn. Stir the kernels into the corn cream mixture, along with salt and pepper to taste. Pour the corn mixture into 10 well-oiled 3 oz molds or a pie dish. Pull one oven rack partially out of the oven. Set the molds in a roasting pan, and place the roasting pan on the pulled-out rack. Carefully pour the boiling water from the kettle into the roasting pan, being careful not to get any water in the flan. Carefully push the rack back into the oven. Bake until the flan is firm, about 40 minutes. Refrigerate the flan overnight; it's best when it's allowed to fully chill after baking.

For the shrimp, toss them with the paprika and olive oil and marinate for at least 2 hours (shrimp can marinate overnight if necessary).

Just before serving, unmold the flan and cut it into 10 wedges, if you've used 1 pie dish. Put a wedge of flan on each of 10 plates. Let stand at room temperature to warm up slightly before serving.

Meanwhile, make the succotash. Remove the kernels from the remaining three ears of corn. In a large skillet, sauté the corn and peas in half of the butter. Once they have softened slightly, add the red pepper and shallot. When the shallot is translucent, add the wine to the skillet and let it bubble to deglaze the skillet. Swirl in the remaining butter until it melts and sprinkle with green onion. Keep the succotash warm.

Meanwhile, season the shrimp with salt and pepper to taste. Preheat the barbecue to high (400°F). Grill the shrimp just until pink and firm, 2 to 3 minutes on each side.

For the bacon vinaigrette, fry the bacon in a large skillet. Once it's all nearly crispy, add the shallots and garlic and remove the skillet from the heat. Let the mixture cool slightly, then whisk in the sherry vinegar, and season with salt and pepper to taste. Keep the vinaigrette warm.

To serve, spoon the succotash around each serving of flan. Add three shrimp to each plate. Drizzle the warm bacon vinaigrette over the top.

ROASTED FIELD CARROTS WITH POMEGRANATE AND CHÈVRE

CHEF ELLIOT REYNOLDS

Aaron Armstrong, the owner of Blue Wheelbarrow Farm, prides himself on his picture-perfect carrots, so I thought this dish was ideal to showcase his products. For me, this dish is really about putting a great ingredient centre stage and treating it correctly, with a few very simple garnishes or added textures. This is a great salad for early fall, or really any time at all. Sommelier Laura Borutski's choice to pair with this recipe is the 2014 JCR Chardonnay from Rosehall Run. The wine has oak notes that linger and deepen the earthy flavours of the roasted carrots. Being a bright Chardonnay, it jumps with the tartness of the chèvre, its hints of tropical flavours enhance the pomegranate seeds and, overall, the wine gives the dish a light and smoky finish.

Serves 6

ROASTED CARROTS

1 lb (500 g) carrots with leaves (in a variety of colours, if possible)

1 Tbsp olive oil

1 Tbsp honey

5 to 6 sprigs fresh thyme

Salt and freshly ground black pepper

HONEY DRESSING

2 Tbsp olive oil

1 Tbsp cider vinegar

1 Tbsp honey

Salt and freshly ground black pepper

TO SERVE

2 oz (60 g) Fifth Town plain chèvre

3 Tbsp whole milk

Salt and freshly ground white pepper

2 Tbsp pomegranate seeds

2 Tbsp hazelnuts, toasted and roughly chopped

12 fresh dill sprigs

For the roasted carrots, preheat the oven to 350°F. Rinse the carrots, then blanch them whole in a pot of boiling, salted water for 2 to 3 minutes. Immediately transfer the carrots to a bowl of ice water to cool.

Once the carrots have cooled, place them on a baking sheet lined with parchment paper. Drizzle with olive oil and honey and scatter with thyme, and salt and pepper to taste, then toss well. Roast the carrots until tender, 30 to 45 minutes, depending on their thickness. Remove from the oven and let cool.

For the honey dressing, whisk together the olive oil, vinegar, honey, and salt and pepper to taste.

Just before serving, combine the chèvre and milk in the top half of a double boiler or in a bowl set over a saucepan of hot, not boiling water. Stir the chèvre until smooth and spreadable. Remove from the heat and season with salt and pepper to taste.

Slice the carrots lengthwise in half or quarters (depending on size) and toss with most of the honey dressing, reserving a little of the dressing to finish the dish.

Using a spoon, spread the chèvre on a serving plate. Arrange the carrots over the chèvre. Garnish with the pomegranate seeds, hazelnuts and dill. Drizzle the reserved dressing over the top.

ASPARAGUS WITH RHUBARB BEURRE BLANC, RADISHES & MIZUNA

CHEF JONATHAN PONG, DRAKE DEVONSHIRE, WELLINGTON

In the summer when the county is in full bloom and roadside farm stalls are full of beautiful vegetables, it's hard not to be inspired by all that it has to offer. Asparagus and rhubarb are some of the vegetables that pop up early in the season. I feel that they're a natural pairing, the tart flavoured rhubarb contrasting with the vegetal dark green asparagus.

Dodie Ellenbogen operates a fantastic farm outside of Picton. She's been supplying the Drake Devonshire with incredible vegetables every season. Her mizuna and radishes both have a nice hint of spiciness, and the sweetness of the butter in the rhubarb beurre blanc sauce brings it all together. The County Cider makes for a refreshing pairing. I really like the bright crisp notes of the cider, as it helps refresh the palate.

Serves 4

4 stalks rhubarb, trimmed of leaves and washed	Sea salt, to taste
½ shallot	1 bunch asparagus, trimmed and washed
2 Tbsp white wine	¼ cup + 1 Tbsp butter, diced and kept cold
1 Tbsp honey	2 radishes, thinly sliced
1 Tbsp olive oil	Mizuna leaves, for garnish

Chop three of the rhubarb stalks into small pieces. Place in a juicer or blender and process until smooth. Strain the rhubarb through fine mesh strainer so that all the pulp is removed. With the remaining stalk, finely dice it and set aside.

Finely dice the shallot and place in a small pan along with the white wine. Cook over medium heat until the wine reduces by half, about 3 minutes. Add the honey and ¼ cup of the rhubarb juice to the pan (there will be extra rhubarb juice left over, which you can drink or serve over ice cream). Continue cooking on medium heat until the mixture has reduced by two-thirds.

While rhubarb juice is reducing, preheat

the barbecue to high (400°F). Lightly oil the asparagus and season with salt. Place on the barbecue and cook for about 3 to 4 minutes, until lightly charred but still crisp. Remove the asparagus from grill and set aside.

Add the cubes of butter into the pan with the rhubarb, and stir constantly until melted and slightly thickened. Do not over-heat the mixture or the butter will split out of the sauce. Taste and adjust the seasoning with salt. Remove from the heat and stir in the finely diced rhubarb.

Plate the grilled asparagus and spoon the rhubarb beurre blanc overtop. Garnish with sliced radishes and a few leaves of mizuna.

SMOKED TOMATO SAUCE

CHEF CHRIS WYLIE, THE MANSE BOUTIQUE INN, PICTON

I use this delicious smoked tomato sauce on lots of dishes, from salads to fish, but mostly I use it for breakfast. It's especially good with some simple poached eggs, served on locally-made good hearth bread. When smoking tomatoes, I use a mixture of wood chips: apple, cherry, hickory and Jack Daniels, but feel free to use whatever you've got on hand or are on sale at your local hardware store.

Serves 4

6 vine-ripened tomatoes

¼ medium yellow onion, diced

2 to 3 cloves garlic, chopped

1 Tbsp granulated sugar

⅓ cup red wine vinegar

1 cup vegetable oil

Salt and freshly ground black pepper, to taste

TO SERVE

Poached eggs

Thick-cut bacon or salmon gravlax

Good-quality bread

Microgreens

SPECIAL EQUIPMENT:

Smoker, wood chips

To smoke the tomatoes, first soak 2 cups of wood chips in cold water for 1 hour. Reserve another cup of dry wood chips.

Preheat half of the barbecue to medium heat (350°F), and line a baking tray that will fit on the top rack of your barbecue with parchment paper.

Spread a large piece of aluminum foil on your counter, and place 1 cup of the dry wood chips overtop. Place the 2 cups of soaked wood chips over the dry chips, and then roll up the long ends of the aluminum foil to make a log. Leave the short ends at either side of the log open and tilted up.

Place the vine-ripened tomatoes on the prepared baking tray and place that on the top rack of your barbecue, away from the direct heat of the grill. Place the wood chip log right on the grill, over the flames and under the tomatoes.

Smoke the tomatoes for 1 to 1½ hours, or until the tomatoes have rendered off some of their water and the juices have

caramelized on the parchment paper. The tomatoes should look charred when they're ready.

Remove the baking tray from the barbecue, and lightly rub the tomatoes on the tray to release the skins and encourage the smoky flavour. Set the tomatoes aside.

When you're ready to serve, blend the smoked tomatoes and their caramelized juices with the onions, garlic, sugar and red wine vinegar. Purée until smooth. With the blender running, slowly add the vegetable oil in a steady stream to emulsify the dressing. Season to taste with salt and pepper. This dressing can be made ahead, and stored in the fridge for up to 1 week.

Serve the sauce drizzled over poached eggs on toasted bread, with thick-cut bacon or smoked salmon on the side. Garnish with microgreens.

APPLE GALETTE

CHEF MICHAEL SULLIVAN, MERRILL INN, PICTON

By late fall, the county is chockablock with fresh apples. If you buy the right variety and store them properly, you can enjoy fresh local apples throughout the winter. Here's a recipe for a popular winter dessert we serve along with a scoop of the Merrill Inn's own cinnamon ice cream. Edward Shubert, one of the inn's owners, suggests pairing the galette with Huff Estates Off-Dry Riesling or County Cider Company's Iced Cider. Both would pair wonderfully, but the Riesling has a nice acidity level which will cut the natural sweetness of the baked apples.

Serves 12

DOUGH

2 cups cake-and-pastry flour

½ tsp table salt

½ tsp granulated sugar

¾ cup cold unsalted butter, cut in ¼-inch (6 mm) pieces

¾ cup cold water

APPLE FILLING

5 large, tart baking apples, such as Northern Spy, Crispin or Golden Delicious

2 Tbsp cold unsalted butter, cut in ¼-inch (6 mm) pieces

3 Tbsp granulated sugar

¼ cup apricot preserves

For the dough, sift the flour, salt and sugar into a large bowl. Add the butter to the flour mixture, and cut it in with a pastry cutter until the pieces of butter are smaller, but still visible. Sprinkle in the cold water and mix with a fork until just combined. Do not overmix.

Turn the dough out on to the countertop (don't flour the countertop). Starting with the dough farthest away from you, smear a small amount of the dough against the counter with the heel of your hand. Continue this process until all the dough has been smeared against the countertop.

Gather the dough together, turn it through 90 degrees and repeat the smearing process. Wrap the dough tightly in plastic wrap and refrigerate for at least 1 hour.

Once the dough has rested, roll it out on a lightly floured surface to a 13-inch (33 cm) disc. Tuck about ½ inch (1 cm) of the outer edge underneath all round to make it a little thicker (like a pizza crust).

Carefully transfer the dough to a large baking sheet lined with parchment paper. Preheat the oven to 400°F.

Next, prepare the apples for the topping. Peel, core, halve the apples, then cut them into ⅛-inch (3 mm) slices.

Arrange the apples on the dough, placing them in a circle around the outer edge, then moving inward in an overlapping, scalloped pattern, until the dough is completely covered. Dot the apples with the butter and sprinkle with granulated sugar.

Bake until the apples are tender and caramelized and the crust is golden brown and thoroughly cooked, 45 to 60 minutes.

In a small saucepan, heat the apricot preserves with a few tablespoonfuls of water until it is runny. Strain the apricot preserves into a small bowl, discarding the solids in the sieve. Brush the hot galette with the hot strained preserves.

Slide the galette onto a cutting board and cut into wedges while still warm. Serve with cinnamon or your favourite ice cream.

Chris Wylie

Rebecca Hunt

Jonathan Pong

Elliot Reynolds

Jamie Kennedy

Cynthia Peters

Andreas Feller

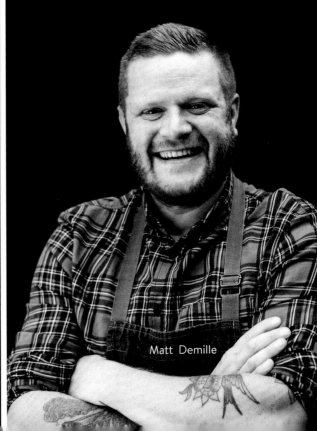
Matt Demille

Meghan Van Horne

Michael Sullivan

Neil Dowson

Lili Sullivan

Scott Royce

TASTEMAKER PROFILE

◇◇◇◇◇◇◇◇◇◇◇◇◇◇◇◇◇◇◇◇◇◇

County FM | "The Voice of the County"

Deb Simpson's always had a unique perspective on Prince Edward County. "My husband and I would sail into Picton Bay and admire it from the water. That was more than 25 years ago. We always talked about buying a house here, but instead we'd buy a bottle of wine and forget about it."

In 2006, Simpson and her husband, Treat Hull, finally bought that house and although they've lived here a relatively short time, they've already made a significant impact. Treat was instrumental in helping to bring community radio to the island, and today, Deb is the general manager of County FM, the much-loved broadcaster.

It would be hard to overstate how quickly the station, with its mix of music, news and information, has become a vital part of life. With five part-time and four full-time staff, and 85 volunteers, the station brings 40 programs a week to the air. More than half the people in the county who listen to the radio at all listen to County FM every day. Those are numbers that any station would be proud of.

"The idea of a community radio station percolated for years," Simpson says, "but it wasn't until 2011 when Gary

Mooney convened a dozen people for a meeting that the idea gathered momentum. We came up with a mandate to fund and operate a not-for-profit radio station that reflects and contributes to the richness, diversity, public safety and economic vitality of Prince Edward County."

They established a board, an eclectic mix of notable locals: HAM operator Doug Monk, former CRTC executive Peter Fleming, broadcaster John Mather, lawyer Sheila Mathers, True North Records founder Bernie Finkelstein, broadcaster Terry Culbert, and the Acoustic Grill's Steve Purtell. Legendary broadcaster JJ Johnson came onboard for the first year.

It took three years from the initial meeting until County FM received its licence in 2014. By October of that year, the station was live. "It was right in the middle of a municipal election," Deb recalls. "We hit the ground running."

"One comment we get," Deb says, "is people telling us they never knew how much was going on in the county. They'd be in their own little area and wouldn't know what was happening in Sophiasburgh or North Marysburgh or even in Wellington. Those kinds of comments make us really happy."

Appendix

TOURISM BOARDS & ONLINE RESOURCES

PRINCE EDWARD COUNTY
Festivals & Celebrations
*http://prince-edward-county.com
/festivals-celebrations/*
Calendar of Events
*http://prince-edward-county.com
/event/*

BAY OF QUINTE
Tourism Board
www.bayofquinte.com

AMELIASBURGH
Tourism Board
www.ameliasburgh.com

BLOOMFIELD
Tourism Board
*www.bloomfieldontario.ca |
info@bloomfieldontario.ca*
Calendar of Events
www.bloomfieldontario.ca/events

CARRYING PLACE
[See Prince Edward County]

CHERRY VALLEY
[See Prince Edward County]

CONSECON
Official Website
www.consecon.ca

DEMORESTVILLE
[See Prince Edward County]

GLENORA
[See Prince Edward County]

HILLIER
[See Prince Edward County]

LAKE ON THE MOUNTAIN
Provincial Park
296 County Road 7 Picton, ON
K0K 2T0 | (613) 393-3319 |
*www.ontarioparks.com/park
/lakeonthemountain*

MILFORD
[See Prince Edward County]

NORTHPORT
[See Prince Edward County]

PICTON

Visitor Information

208 Main Street, Suite 103, Picton, ON
K0K 2T0 | (613) 476-7901 Ext. 211 |
www.experiencepicton.com
Calendar of Events
www.experiencepicton.com/events

REDNERSVILLE

[See Prince Edward County]

SOPHIASBURGH

[See Prince Edward County]

WAUPOOS

[See Prince Edward County]

WAUPOOS ISLAND

[See Prince Edward County]

WELLINGTON

Tourism Board
www.discoverwellington.ca

DIRECTIONS

◇◇◇◇◇◇◇◇◇◇◇◇◇◇◇◇◇◇◇◇◇◇◇◇

BY CAR

From Toronto

- Take ON-401 E (90 minutes) to Exit 522
- Right on County Road 40 (5 minutes) toward Trenton
- Right on County Road 33/Loyalist Parkway (10 minutes)
- Continue on County Road 33/ Loyalist Parkway

From Ottawa

- Take ON-416 S toward ON-401 (40 minutes)
- Merge onto ON-401 W

- Take ON-401 W TO Exit 566 (100 minutes)
- Take Exit 566 and turn left on County Road 15/Marysville Road (5 minutes)
- Continue straight onto County Road 49 (20 minutes)
- Veer right onto County Road 33/ Loyalist Parkway (10 minutes)

From Montreal

- Take ON-401 W (3 hours) to exit 566
- Take Exit 566 and turn left on County Road 15/Marysville Road (5 minutes)

- Continue straight onto County
  Road 49 (20 minutes)
- Veer right onto County Road 33/
  Loyalist Parkway (10 minutes)

BY GLENORA FERRY (FREE CAR FERRY)

About the ferry
- On Highway 33, between Lake on
  the Mountain and Adolphustown
- (613) 540-5131 | www.mto.gov.on.ca
  /english/ontario-511/ferries.
  shtml#glenora
- Spring schedule (Victoria Day
  through late June): Every 30 minutes, Monday through Friday, 6
  a.m. through 1.15 a.m., and on
  weekends, 6 a.m. through 10 a.m.
  and 7.30 p.m. through 1.15 a.m.;
  every 15 minutes on weekends,
  10.15 a.m. through 7.30 p.m.
- Summer schedule (late June through
  mid-October): Every 30 minutes, 6
  a.m. through 10 a.m. and 7.30 p.m.
  through 1.15 a.m.; every 15 minutes,
  10.15 a.m. through 7.30 p.m.
- Winter schedule (mid-October
  through Friday before Victoria
  Day): Every 30 minutes, 6 a.m.
  through 1.15 a.m.

Directions from dock
- Take County Road 33/Loyalist
  Parkway

BUS

From Toronto
- Greyhound 5360, 5862, 5858 to
  Belleville, Ontario ($30-40 |
  3 hours, 30 minutes | 1 time/day)

From Ottawa
- Greyhound 5359, 5859 to Belleville,
  Ontario ($40-50 | 3 hours, 40 min-
  utes | 1 time/day)

Directions from bus station
- Take a taxi to Prince Edward
  County (40 minutes)

TRAIN

Belleville Station
- Serviced by Via Rail trains running
  between Toronto and Kingston,
  Ottawa and Montreal

Directions from train station
- Take a taxi to Prince Edward
  County (40 minutes)

CALENDAR OF EVENTS

◇◇◇◇◇◇◇◇◇◇◇◇◇◇◇◇◇◇◇◇◇◇◇◇◇◇◇◇◇◇◇◇◇◇◇◇

JANUARY
- Milford Winter Carnival | *jcmleewis@kos.net*

FEBRUARY
- Sophiasburgh Winter Carnival | *www.facebook.com/Sophiasburgh-Recreation-Committee*
- Winterfest at Sandbanks | *www.facebook.com/friendsofsandbanks*

MARCH
- Maple in the County (maple syrup festival) | *www.mapleinthecounty.ca*
- Spring Countylicious (a celebration of culinary experiences) | *www.countylicious.com*

APRIL
- The County Reads (local residents champion a book of their choice, with audience voting) | *www.pecauthorfest.com/event/county-reads*
- Prince Edward County Authors Festival (celebrates Canadian literature and emerging writers) | *www.pecauthorfest.com*
- Waterfall Tour | *www.prince-edward-county.com/item/waterfall-tours/*

MAY
- Walleye World Live Release Fishing Derby | *www.kiwaniswalleyeworld.com/*
- County Pop Community Music Festival | *www.countypop.com*
- Spring Birding Festival | *www.peptbo.ca/coming-events-p43.php*
- Terroir Wine Celebration (taste-test the new season's wines) | *www.countyterroir.ca*
- Quinte's Isle Bluegrass Celebration | *www.quintebluegrass.com*
- Terroir Run (11 km marathon in wine country) | *www.terroirrun.com/*

JUNE
- The Great Canadian Cheese Festival | *www.cheesefestival.ca*
- Uncork Canada (wine festival) | *www.uncorkcanada.ca/*
- Art in the County (art festival) | *www.artinthecounty.com/*
- Canada Day in Wellington (two-day festival featuring street dancing, fireworks, a parade and music)

JULY
- Canada Day in Picton (features a large celebration and fireworks)

- Great Ontario Salmon Derby (July–August) | *www.greatontario salmonderby.ca*
- Lavender Festival at Prince Edward County Lavender Farm | *www.peclavender.com*
- Music at Port Milford Festival | *www.musicatportmilford .org/2017performances*
- Bloomfield Soapbox Derby | *http://bloomfieldontario.ca/events/*

AUGUST

- Classical Unbound Music Festival | *www.classicalunbound.com*
- Dragon Boat Festival in Wellington | *www.e-clubhouse.org/sites /wellingtonon/page-7.php*
- Festival Players of Prince Edward County (local theatre) | *www.festivalplayers.ca*
- PEX Country Music Jamboree | (613) 476-6535
- Prince Edward Auto Club Street Meet (classic cars on display) | (613) 813- 4596
- Prince Edward County Jazz Festival | *www.pecjazz.org*

SEPTEMBER

- Rednersville Road Art Tour | www.rednersvilleroadarttour.com
- Women Killing It (crime writing festival) | *www.womenkillingitauthors festival.wordpress.com*

- Heirloom Hurrah (tomato tasting) | *www.vickisveggies.com/events.html*
- Picton Fair (agricultural fair) | *www.pictonfair.org*
- Live 50s & 60s Rock 'n' Roll Festival | (613) 476-6535
- Red, White & Blues (music festival) | *www.redwhiteandblues.ca*
- Classical Music Festival | *www.pecmusicfestival.com*
- Sandbanks Music Festival | *www.sandbanksmusicfest.com*
- Milford Fair (the biggest little fair in the county) | *www.southmarysburghmirror.com /community/milford-fair*
- Ameliasburgh Fall Fair | *www.ameliasburgh.com/fallfair*
- Taste! Community Grown (wine and culinary festival) | *www.tastecommunitygrown.com*
- Artists' Studio Tour | *www.pecstudiotour.com*

OCTOBER

- County Marathon (full marathon) | *www.thecountymarathon.ca*
- Pumpkinfest | *www.pec.on.ca /pumpkinfest*
- Fall Countylicious (a celebration of culinary experiences) | *www.countylicious.com*

NOVEMBER

- The Maker's Hand (artisan show) | *www.themakershand.com*
- Firelight Lantern Festival | *www.firelightfest.blogspot.ca*
- Wassail (celebration of the wine harvest) | *www.princeedward countywine.ca/wassail*
- Consecon Santa Claus Parade | *www.consecon.ca*
- Picton Santa Claus Parade | *www.facebook.com /PictonSantaClausParade*
- Bloomfield Festival of Lights | *www.bloomfieldontario.ca*
- Festival of Trees (silent auction and entertainment) | (613) 476-2181

DECEMBER

- Christmas House Tour (a tour of heritage buildings decorated in Christmas finery) | *sheltonpeta@gmail.com*
- Ameliasburgh's Christmas in the Village | *museums@pecounty.on.ca*

FURTHER READING

Campbell, Steve, Janet Davies, and Ian S. Robertson, *Prince Edward County: An Illustrated History* (Bloomfield: County Magazine Printshop Limited, 2009)

Crawford, Douglas A., *County Canners: A History of the Canning Industry in Prince Edward County* (Bloomfield: County Magazine Printshop Limited, 2003)

Cruickshank, Tom, Peter John Stokes, and John de Visser, *The Settler's Dream: A Pictorial History of the Older Buildings of Prince Edward County* (Picton: Corporation of the County of Prince Edward County, 1984)

French, Orland, *Wind, Water, Barley & Wine: The Nature of Prince Edward County* (Bellville: Wallbridge House Publishing, 2013)

"History Lives Here," History Lives Here INC, accessed May 9, 2017, http://historyliveshere.ca.

Hunt, C.W., *Rumrunners of the County: Including Gamblers of the County* (Bloomfield: County Magazine Printshop Limited, 2006)

Lunn, Richard, and Janet Lunn, *The County: The First Hundred Years in Loyalist Prince Edward* (Picton: Prince Edward County Council, 1967)

"Prince Edward County Historical Society," Prince Edward County Historical Society, accessed May 9, 2017, https://pehistsoc.wordpress.com

Robertson, Ian S., *Camp Picton: Wartime to Peacetime* (Bloomfield: County Magazine Printshop Limited, 2013)

Robertson, Ian S., *The Monarch of Main Street: The Birth, Decline and Rebirth of Picton's Regent Theatre* (Bloomfield: County Magazine Printshop Limited, 2014)

Sharpe, Robert J., *The Lazier Murder: Prince Edward County, 1884* (Toronto: University of Toronto Press, 2011)

ACKNOWLEDGEMENTS

From Chris:

Thanks to all the excellent people whose brilliance, dedication and love of the county make it such a special place. Thanks in particular to Krista, David, Rebecca, Andrew and Alex, the most generous hosts a writer could hope for. Johnny for capturing the beauty of the county in pictures, and introducing me to so many wonderful locals. Thanks to the team at *Food & Drink* for first giving me a chance to write about the county. And to everyone at Appetite by Random House and Penguin Random House Canada: Zoe for her unflagging enthusiasm and big picture perspective. Brad, Robert, Leah, Bonnie, Susan and Carla who recognized that the county warranted a big, beautiful book and conspired to make it a reality.

From Johnny:

I would like to thank my parents, William and Margaret, for their love and courage in bringing the family from Hong Kong to a new life in Canada three decades ago. My extended family, Matthew, Liz and Thora in Waupoos, and Kyle and Jenny in Picton. My Libra twin, Alex Fida, for your continual support and ongoing effort to preserve history and restore beauty. Ruth Gangbar for your food styling magic. All the talented farmers in the county for feeding everyone with back-breaking hard work. All my hospitality industry friends working tirelessly and sacrificing your weekends to bring visitors the best county experience. My friends at Norman Hardie, Hinterland, County Road Beer, The Grange, Closson Chase, The Old Third, Long Dog and many other wineries and breweries. My chef friends: Neil, Chris, Scott, Matty, Cynthia, Elliot, Henry, Jamie, Rebecca, Paul and all the others who dedicate their life and passion to cooking good food. My comrade Chris Johns for your wizardly words. My editor Zoe Maslow for taking care of business with the best sense of humour. Big thank you to Appetite by Random House for making this book a reality: Brad Martin, Robert McCullough, Leah Springate, Bonnie Maitland, Susan Burns and Carla Kean. Last but not least, thank you to my beautiful wife, Kate, for all your love, support and patience, always.

MAIN INDEX

RECIPES INDEX